Wacky Days:

How To Get Millions Of $$$ In Free Publicity By Creating A "Real" Holiday & Other Tactics Used by Media Experts

By

T.S. "Tom" Peric'

Gregson & Lestrade, Publishers, Cherry Hill, NJ

Wacky Days: How To Get Millions Of $$$ In Free Publicity By Creating A "Real" Holiday & Other Tactics Used By Media Experts

By

T.S. "Tom" Peric'

Published by:

Gregson & Lestrade, Publishers
2040 Fairfax Avenue
Cherry Hill, NJ 08003
(856) 874-0049
(856) 874-0052 (Fax)

ISBN: 0-9726219-0-3
Printed in the United States of America

Library of Congress Cataloging-in-Publication
Library of Congress Control Number: 2003114338

Table Of Contents

This book is dedicated to those individuals, businesses and organizations that have a message, product or service with a story, but don't know how to get the media to pay attention to their tale.

A Matter of Gender

The issue of how to refer to gender is still the subject of debate by those who write. I dislike **he/she** and run from **s/he** (it sounds like some evil creature from the black lagoon). Using "he and she" throughout the book becomes tiresome and has a certain air of political correctness which I find irritating. I'm not sure which approach to use so that everyone is satisfied and no one is offended. A task that is usually impossible anyway. Until I find a better alternative, I've generally remained with the traditional "he" to imply both genders.

HVALA

Or

▪ A Thank-You Note

There are several persons who played an important role in the writing of *Wacky Days*. First, and without a doubt, foremost, is my friend, Adams Hudson, president of Montgomery, Ala.-based, Hudson, Ink. I met him at Penton Media's Comfortech show in Atlanta after sitting in during one of his seminars. I love watching other speakers deliver their speeches and presentations. Adams knew his material "cold" and he could deliver it with charm, wit and insight. While he doesn't make a living as a *professional* speaker, he's better than most. I guess it's natural ability. We've become friends and each other's adviser. He's also a great advertising guy. He's expensive but worth every dollar (www.hudsonink.com).

At that seminar, he shamed me into writing a book without realizing it. He had written a book which sold-out at the seminar. It was a 50-page manual, *Low-Cost, High Response Marketing*. It was worth every penny, but it certainly wasn't a BIG book. I picked it up and thought, "I could do this." After all, I had spent more than 22 years as a journalist and had written a thesis in graduate school that exceeded the thickness of his book. Actually, he adhered to the rule that everyone should follow when writing: Write what you have to say, then stop. Adams did and I did, too. I clearly needed a push past the tripwire. That push was Adams Hudson. Thanks, guy.

I would also like to thank Milka Peric' for her busy markings on my first draft. She not only caught all the gaffes – and there were so many I often winced – but she was always ready to say: "I don't understand this, it isn't clear or what do you mean?" She's given my business a great boost by helping me with all my communications. And she gave me invaluable editing help, at all hours of the day or night, at the family rate, when I started the business. I am forever thankful.

Also, a large dose of thanks goes to Mary Morvan, president of Talbot Drake Inc. (www.talbotdrake.com), who is the kind of consultant (though she hates the word) that I want to be when I grow up. Her assistance, advice and support have meant a great deal to me especially in my fledgling days when money and successes were few. There is no one I would rather talk about business with than this top-notch consultant. She's also the Darth Vader of the retail advertising business. Some *very* big clients come to her to save money. She saves them *millions*. I'm proud of my little sister.

Special thanks must go to Kathie Dixon for a superb job on designing the pages of Wacky Days and to Leslie A. Thompson Barni for her creative touch on the book's cover design.

I'd like to thank supreme publicist, George A. Becker, who in a moment of uncommon friendship, showed me how he writes a proposal for a client when I was making my first such endeavor. He did this knowing full well that I would become a competitor.

Thanks must also go to John Tidyman and Michele Beight who introduced me to my first clients. While I had to close the deal, without them, I would never have had the opportunity of meeting and representing two well-known clients.

Additionally, I must thank Tim Mueller and Dan Rose, who as I understand, recently sold their very successful company. Despite a busy schedule, they met me for lunch while I was unemployed and just beginning to cautiously think about forming my own public relations firm. We were in The Flats for lunch (they paid) as they examined my resume. They asked me what I intended to charge for my services and their bemusement was obvious at the low rate I volunteered. Both cautioned me against it. They suggested that with my background, I should double my rate. I walked away from that luncheon and fortunately followed their advice. Their counsel gave me a far more advanced starting line than I would have drawn on my own. I must also thank Lou Reyes, Jr. for providing me with projects to help stimulate cash flow in those early days.

I have never forgotten the generosity these individuals showed me without ever asking for anything in return.

Finally, a special word of thanks to Chris. He's the master editor and arbiter of everything that I write if it's important enough for others to read. Chris has been editing my work for more than a decade (poor fellow) and I know that whatever compliments I receive for my work, is in great part directly attributed to his skill at making me a tighter and brighter writer. I hope we have a few more decades together.

Chapter 1

Does This Publicity Stuff *Really* Make A Difference

A True Story

As a young reporter in Washington, D. C., in the late 1970s, I was researching the background of a publication called *The Contest Newsletter* A friend and I went to an organization near my office in the National Press Building, and I looked at a newsletter on newsletters (Yes, Virginia, they do exist). There, in black and white, it indicated that the *Kiplinger Newsletter* had fallen to the No. 2 spot. At the top of the circulation heap was, as I remember it, *The Contest Newsletter*, with more than one million subscribers. At $19.95 for a one-year subscription, you could consider that a fairly expensive publication back then. (Especially when you realized that it only consisted of about 12 pages, 8½ X 11 inches with no photographs or drawings.) It simply listed various contests you could enter for free by following guidelines issued by the various companies. Contrary to popular belief, you didn't need an official coupon or entry blank. A small, blank sheet of paper with your name and address usually sufficed.

Let's see, one million subscribers at $19.95 and . . . well, the math's pretty easy. The expense is mostly fulfillment, paper and postage. Whew, what a profit maker.

But what most people don't know is that this newsletter zoomed to the head of the class because of **FREE** publicity.

The two owners of the newsletter at the time it reached its zenith were a husband-and-wife team, who bought the newsletter from its founder in Texas. When they bought it, it had a nice, small, manageable circulation of about 20,000. Not a bad little business, one that would make most of us happy and proud.

The wife in this family business sent a notice to a national magazine offering a free copy of the newsletter to anyone who wanted one. All they had to do was include a self-addressed, stamped envelope (SASE). When the magazine came out, this offer appeared as a tiny, one-paragraph item. It was NOT an ad nor was it an article and it certainly didn't have particular pizzazz.

The item ran in *Family Circle*, which had a huge circulation, in the millions. After it ran the item, about 10,000 requests came in asking for free samples of the newsletter. "We were overwhelmed," said the owner. That single mention in a magazine brought in potential subscribers equaling half of the newsletter's circulation. Not surprisingly, many of those who requested a sample copy converted and became subscribers.

But the owners of *The Contest Newsletter* learned a valuable lesson. Free mention in magazines, especially large national publications offering a free sample, could introduce their product to potential subscribers. Plus, it cost the owners **NOTHING**, except for the free sample they sent out. There's little doubt the owners were fortunate that they had the right product. At the time, there was only one other newsletter, to my knowledge, devoted to contests. Also, their product had universal appeal. Most people like the idea of entering contests for free, hoping to win prizes simply by filling out (in most cases) their name and address on a small piece of paper. Nothing could be easier, and this was before you were able to purchase lottery tickets on every corner. Besides, lottery tickets cost money, but most legitimate contests are free, and that's why they remain popular.

The key, however, to the wild success of this newsletter was that free, national publicity. It turned a true mom-and-pop operation from a part-time income to a business that grossed somewhere in the vicinity of $20 million annually. According to one of the owners, it was that appearance in *Family Circle*, and subsequent appearances in other magazines, that catapulted this tiny business into a multimillion-dollar enterprise. Mention of their newsletter in publications boosted the requests for free sample copies, which in turn, drove up subscriptions. I love this story because it's Horatio Alger in real life (poor guy makes it big) and also because it's true.

How do I know this story is true? Because I interviewed one of the owners of the newsletter and wrote a story about how to win contests. (A champ at winning contests told me the secret is the three P's: Paper, Postage and Persistence. I even began entering contests myself for a short time, winning small cash prizes, a hair dryer and a few other items.) I saw a photocopy of that first blurb in *Family Circle*, and it really was a tiny mention. It worked wonders. It's not hyperbole to say, in this example, that free publicity was worth millions.

A True Story: An architectural firm in the late 1990s was starting to grow again as it drew near its 40th anniversary. Previously, it had grown to more than 75 employees and then faltered to about half that figure during the real estate crash of the late '80s. Now they were off the ropes and making their moves again. This time around, they wanted publicity, without spending a lot of money for it. On average, they might have received about $20,000 in annual media coverage with no effort except keeping the door open. That means, if you took the free editorial coverage they received and bought an equal amount of advertising, it might have equaled $20,000 annually. And that is a generous estimate.

This architectural firm got aggressive. They went to a fellow who was new in the publicity or public relations field but had been a longtime journalist who knew how the media work. (From here on, consider the words publicity and public relations to be interchangeable. The goal is still the same: Getting media coverage without paying for it.) This publicity specialist knew the old adage that placement of stories in the media begins and ends with ideas and people. He also focused on the goal the founder of the company shared with him. The company's goal was not to find its name in the usual consumer magazines or even architectural magazines. The founder, shrewdly, wanted to appear in trade magazines that his clients read. This journalist developed a three-tiered list of trade and general publications. The "A" list was the most important. Indeed, the firm would judge the publicity expert's results, in large part, on how effectively he was able to obtain stories about the company in magazines on this list. He would mine the "B" list of magazines if there was time to pitch them story ideas. Finally, there was the "C" list, which he also could attack if the time ever became available (it didn't).

It took about one year for the publicity plan to swing into full action. When it did, the plan was able to obtain *more than $1.5 million in publicity*. Why? Because the vice president of the firm followed the publicity expert's plan to the letter. She directed a top-notch staff member to implement the nuts-and-bolts aspects of the plan, while the high-level pitching and strategy issues fell on the shoulders of the publicity expert.

Why am I so intimately familiar with the publicity history of this company? I was the publicity consultant they hired to raise the halo around their name. They were both one of my earliest and largest clients. (Large, obviously being a relative term. I now represent several clients whose stock sells on the New York Stock Exchange.)

Boring But Necessary

The next two paragraphs are probably the most boring part of this book, and that's why I'll keep it short. Journalists, or former journalists for that matter, usually feel uncomfortable talking about themselves. After all, they spend a career interviewing people who talk about themselves and their plans, hopes, achievements or mistakes. These interviewees also talk about other people. However, journalists (except for Hunter S. Thompson) don't usually talk or write about themselves. In the ancient days of the typewriter B.C. (Before Computers), it was said that in some newsrooms the old-time editors would prohibit any journalist to type the capital I. This prevented aspiring journalists from referring to themselves in the first person. If you want to know more about me, look at the back of this book. Questions about an author's background are not only fair, they should be posed. My biography will explain my background in detail.

But the most relevant issue that you should know is that I have spent more than two decades as a journalist. I understand what makes a good news story, and I've applied that formula to all my publicity efforts. I continue to serve as the editor of two national trade publications, so I'm still wearing an editor's hat. Finally, I earn 99.99 percent of my income by consulting on editorial or publicity issues. I do what I preach, because I'm in the pew with the parishioners.

I wrote this book and conduct *Publicity For Profit* seminars because I enjoy teaching. Indeed, I spent the first five years of my working life as an instructor before going to college and pursuing a journalism career. I taught courses on writing for years and have now returned to the seminar platform to teach about how to gain publicity. It's a great break from pitching (selling) story ideas to the media about my clients or offering advice about how to make a publication more effective. I enjoy teaching people how to take the mystery out of gaining publicity, and, as an expert involved in the publicity business, I enjoy it when my clients, students and readers of my book succeed, too. The goal every good teacher should have is clear-cut: He wants to make his students better than he is. That's my goal, too. I want you to gain the maximum publicity exposure for yourself. Because I've gotten millions of dollars worth of free publicity for my clients, I hope you have the same good fortune. This book will show you how.

Chapter 2

Publicity Versus Advertising

"C'mon, Nothing's Free!"

A mistake I make occasionally is forgetting that many people don't know the difference between advertising and publicity. Sometimes I just assume that the group of business people I'm talking to understands the distinction. I'm continually surprised that many people actually believe that you pay for articles that appear in newspapers or magazines. These people make no distinction between free publicity (the articles) and advertising. Well, there's a great difference between the two.

Difference No. 1: Money, honey. You pay for advertising, you don't pay for publicity. The cost, or lack of it, is probably the most dramatic difference between advertising and publicity. Advertising can be very expensive to buy and costly to create, and there's no guarantee it will work. I'm not saying that advertising never works, because we can look around us and see that sometimes it does. Just as often, in fact probably more frequently, it doesn't. Either way, it can be very expensive to discover which ad will work (assuming you actually find out). Publicity, on the other hand, costs you nothing if the media outlet "picks up" your story, idea or press release and runs it in its magazine or puts it over the airwaves. (All you must pay for is the cost of writing and distributing the press release, which is usually far less than creating an ad.) You can usually implement a full-blown publicity campaign for peanuts compared to what it would cost to create, produce and run an ad in a publication or on radio or television.

A True Story: I only advertised once. For a swap (I didn't pay for the ad but gave some publicity advice to the publisher), I ran an advertisement in a magazine that covered an industry where the executives certainly understood the benefit of publicity. I ran the ad for one year. The number of phone calls I received was a big, fat ZERO. Yes, my advertising friends will read this and say, "The problem was the ad. It wasn't designed properly, the wording was wrong, or some other technical reason." While I'm not a specialist in advertising, I've written some good advertising campaigns that were successful. If we assume that even in my weakest moments I'd be a C- advertising writer (I'm not, I'm much better), then there would have been at least a pinprick of interest. I never got a single inquiry during that entire year. Thank God I didn't have to pay for the ad. But not ONE inquiry? Had I paid for that advertisement, I would have wasted thousands of dollars.

Spending money on advertising is no guarantee of results. You'll be out the money, sometimes a great deal of it. There's no guarantee that publicity will get results either, but at least it only costs a fraction of what you would spend for advertising. That's the problem with advertising. You *pay* for it. And it can cost a fortune. Additionally, it's far more difficult to find out – inexpensively – what works and what doesn't. In other words, while advertising can work and work very well, you might have to test, test, test. Experts at writing mail-order copy will tell you that you frequently have to test, test, test until you get it right. Which, of course, can bleed you into bankruptcy. Because while you're testing, testing, testing, you're also paying, paying, paying. This is just fine for an overall campaign if you have money. If you don't have the money or would rather use your hard-earned dollars for other issues, then seeking free publicity with incredibly small costs is the way to go.

Difference No. 2: Who's in control here? Control freaks probably love advertising because their ad goes into the publication or over the airwaves exactly as they say it should, barring any issue of law or good taste that might prevent the media outlet from actually running it.

For some people, this control is very important, especially if you're wound up real tight. With advertising, you control the process and product because you, your advertising firm or your cousin, Luther, the graphic artist who's designed a few logos, "creates" the ad.

I'll grant you this: Advertising does allow far greater control over your message. It goes out to your audience in exactly the fashion you wish. With publicity, you have less control over how the media shapes your message. However, if you know what you're doing, you usually can ensure that journalists craft a message consistent with your publicity goals. If you want to advertise, naturally, you and your cousin come up with a few witty, original sentences, create some artwork, run it in a publication and voila, the money rolls in. Right? Not quite. For that control, you give up a great deal of the believability factor that people associate with news stories. People are skeptical of advertising. They are far less skeptical of an article or news broadcast. If supreme control and the willingness to spend money are more important to you, then advertising might be the ideal choice to promote your message. But if you want more believability and little to no cost, publicity wins hands down.

Difference No. 3: Publicity raises you above the maddening crowd because of the believability factor. People tend to believe people who they read about in news stories. Despite our cynical society, we still look for people with whom we might (or must) deal with who exhibit traits such as honesty and fairness. We hope that these people offer reliable, even excellent products and services upon which we can rely. Unless the article has a negative slant, its very appearance in the media suggests that at least some of these elements must be associated with the person, business or organization. It's no accident that whenever a business *does* receive some attention, usually through luck, some businesses or organizations immediately pin the article on the wall somewhere. While most business owners lack the skill and insight to milk the article properly, the fact that owners often display the article shows how much they believe the media coverage validates their business as one that's worth special attention. Every study I've ever heard or read about confirms this: People tend to believe editorial or free-standing articles (or news shows) more than they believe advertising. Use yourself as a test case. Even if you doubt or disbelieve an article or a news report, would you believe it more if it were an advertisement? Do you really believe all those ads?

Difference No. 4: I'm better than you, I'm better than you. Publicity makes you a star, and it leaves your competitor playing catch-up or associated with a lesser role in your field or industry. Publicity raises the identity and awareness of your business or organization above your competition. It puts you at the very least where you want to be: on the short list of everyone who needs your product or service. From a business standpoint this is exactly where you want to be. That means when potential customers need your product or service – insurance, bowling balls, financial advice or a nice dinner – you'll be one of the two, three or four businesses or organizations they consider. Maybe you'll be the only one. You must be honest. Unless you're the ONLY game in town, and few people have such a unique business (except occasionally in their own mind), today's buyers have a plethora of choices. The Internet continues to expand those choices. All of my smart clients – and some of them are *very* smart – agree on this point. What you want is to **ALWAYS** be one of the candidates that comes to mind when someone needs your product or expertise. As one client with a national practice told me: "If we make that short list of candidates each time they have a project, I know we'll close some of those deals." I always loved that comment. Because for most of us, you'll close a number of deals if only because of luck. If you own a restaurant, a tough business if there ever was one, do you want people to find your eatery by randomly skimming through the telephone directory with their index finger under the restaurant section? Or do you want them to find you because you're one of three restaurants they've heard about or read about as having the most exciting menu?

Difference No. 5: Publicity and the Lands' End Effect: Publicity provides opportunity that might not have existed elsewhere. You can't possibly control how people hear about you, what they hear or even IF they hear about your product or service. The more exposure that you enjoy – that is, having your story told in the media – the greater your chance of being able to capitalize on that exposure, because more people are aware of what you offer. I call this the Lands' End Effect. I read about Lands' End as a company for years in the business press (forget about the ads or the catalogs, which, I believe, didn't influence my opinion). I had always read about how great they were as a company, how they stood by their products and would take back merchandise if the customer was dissatisfied and so on. Finally, one day I got a Lands' End catalog in the mail and ordered a single, button-down dress shirt. I thought the price was good, and, after receiving it, the quality satisfied me, too. But at what point, based on the publicity to which Lands' End had exposed me, did I decide to BUY something from the company? I really don't know, and that's precisely my point. You don't know when publicity will affect a decision maker, therefore, you don't know which impression will finally close a deal for you. That's why you must be out there <u>constantly</u> trying to make those impressions on people with publicity. Your task should be clear. To quote a former vice president at General Electric (a company that knows something about marketing and publicity) who went to Microsoft: "You want to make deposits in the mental banks of potential customers." I agree completely.

Difference No. 6: Publicity confers the title of expert. *If I'm to decide a single goal for my client in terms of their publicity challenges, I can narrow it down to a single effort: I want the media to consider my clients to be experts. I also want anyone else with whom they come in contact to consider my clients to be experts.* It's really that straightforward. People have a natural tendency to believe that when the media quotes or interviews someone, they must be an expert. What that person says or believes merits enough attention that the media feels it warrants reporting that expert's views. There is a subtlety here.

This book, *Wacky Days,* is all about taking you from being, in all likelihood, an unrecognized expert and turning you into a recognized expert. You must understand the subtlety in this. I have a friend who was a dynamite criminal defense attorney. He was fantastic as a lawyer and now lectures to wanna-be-great criminal defense attorneys. He's shared the speaking platform with internationally known criminal defense attorney Gerry Spence. I can assure you that if you heard his name, you wouldn't recognize it. That's because he spent his career in Alaska, and none of his cases caught the media's attention outside of his state. This is true of all my "unheralded" experts. You might be just as good *or even better* than your better-known competitors. The difference is that they are recognized experts and you're not. If you want to continue that way, if you wish to remain an unknown, don't bother to finish this book. But if you believe that you have a product, skill or service that deserves an audience, publicity is your shortcut to potential customers, clients or audiences. And it's your expertise, in many cases, that attracts and drives the publicity.

Difference No. 7: Publicity: The final reason you should want publicity. (And the one reason you'll never read about in a book on publicity or public relations.) The reason you should consider basking in the limelight and being thought of as an expert is very uncomplicated: It feels GREAT. We're human, and we want people to pay attention to us, especially when we believe that we have something worthwhile to share. Most of us have an ego, and the public acknowledgement that we're somebody – we're experts – makes us feel better about ourselves. Why shouldn't it? Isn't the joy of achievement heightened when we share it with someone? True, that someone might be only your spouse or significant other or it might be nearly 290 million Americans, so I suppose we can differ on the degree to which we want the limelight. I insist that for most people, a moment in the sunshine of publicity is probably not going to help or hurt your chances for eternal salvation. It might have an impact on your own sense of self-worth, it might impress or delight your family and friends, and hopefully, it will have a measurable impact on your business. I just want you to know that it's OK to feel good about the publicity. I'm not suggesting that you're better because you mastered the art of publicity or that you should conduct your daily affairs with a sense of braggadocio. Nothing is wrong with the public recognition of your expertise or success. Public affirmation, after all, begins with people cooing over us as babies and ends with people saying (we hope) good things about us at our funerals. As long as you don't become intoxicated with publicity, it can be healthy and helpful to your ego and to the bottom line of your business or organization. There is an old adage that all newspaper people learn early on . . . the only time most people appear in the newspaper is when someone writes their obituary. I would urge that you don't wait that long.

If you paid for an advertisement that extolled your virtues, people would lambaste you for having an overripe ego. But when the media chooses to write about you, it's because you deserve it. A little publicity never hurt anyone, and it feels good. Try it.

Chapter 3

Promoting Your Expertise

Discover Why You're An Expert

"I think Joe's an expert."
"You're kidding! I know more than him."
Conversation overheard in a restaurant.

The notion that You Are An Expert is absolutely true for virtually everyone. Often there is only one difference between you and your expertise and other "recognizable experts." The difference? They're recognized everywhere as experts. Or at the very least, people they want to influence – their peers or potential customers and clients – recognize them as experts. You're not recognized.

First, who is an expert is a matter of definition. I'm going to define what an expert is and why you meet the definition. In other words, you're going to find out why **YOU'RE** an expert. Then, I'll explain how to promote your expertise.

There are two definitions of an expert: the dictionary's and mine. My definition is far more realistic, approachable and practical. If you can speak or write about any topic for 30 minutes without pause, you're an expert. That's a loose definition, it's Tom's definition, but it's a good one. (If you're a formalist, Webster defines an expert as "one

with the special skill or knowledge representing mastery of a particular subject.") I'm not saying that you should claim you're the ONLY expert on the subject or the BEST expert in your field. I'm saying that if you're reading this book and want to promote a person, product or service, you are probably an expert, using Tom's definition. If you're discussing your topic, for example, I'm not suggesting that you must deliver a polished speech about your topic that shines with wit, clarity and insight. I'm saying that if you're a car mechanic or a bankruptcy lawyer and you can talk to a friend over coffee about the nature of change in auto engines or the proposed changes in the bankruptcy laws, you are an expert. In a more formal sense, if you have developed a specialty of knowledge by dint of effort, training, education and position, you are an expert. This even includes hobbies.

What's missing in the definition? It's looking in the mirror and saying those magic words: **I am an expert.** Your perception of yourself is (for most people) the most common stumbling block that you must overcome if you wish to wear the mantle of an expert. Unless you have an overt ego the size of an oversized watermelon, you probably don't wake up each morning as you stare at the mirror saying, "I'm an expert." But you must develop the self-acceptance and confidence and overcome your reluctance and modesty if you wish to promote yourself. When the media interview someone, do you actually believe that a firefighter, lawyer or bricklayer is the best in his field in the entire United States? Or even in the state? Or even in the city? They're experts, in most cases, because the media is interviewing them and, in a sense, anointing them as an expert. If that expert is in the same field as you, they might actually know less than you. (This is reminiscent of that old joke about doctors. What do you call the person who graduated last in his class in medical school? "Doctor.") The only thing that matters is that an expert knows more than the general public and can convey the necessary information. I know this sounds like harping, but it's absolutely true. The perception battle is one that you must overcome if you're going to promote yourself, your business or your organization. It's one thing that you must accomplish for yourself. I can tell you, as I have, how vital it is to flick on this emotional or psychological mental switch about yourself as an expert. It's up to you to actually do it.

Because I often like to use restaurant examples, let me illustrate. (I don't have any restaurant clients, and the business is inordinately difficult in which to succeed – that's why it makes a great example.) Let's assume that you've been cooking for more than 20 years, you've taken some cooking classes, experimented with a few dishes, traveled each year and met with various chefs to discuss recipes with them. You might even belong to two national "chef" associations, and you've written a sketchy outline of an (unpublished) book with your favorite recipes. Add to this, you teach cooking classes at an adult learning center and operate a successful restaurant. Let's see: You're an expert on cooking (you're a chef) and you're an expert on running a restaurant. Now you have two areas of expertise. All these activities, over time, have developed your knowledge and, therefore, your expertise. Do you really think that someone "off the street" or someone who dabbles a bit in cooking is really going to know more about cooking and meal preparation than you? It would be almost impossible. No one gets a degree in being an expert. They just are one. They have someone anoint them as experts. Why shouldn't that someone be you?

I happen to be an expert on publicity. Though I've immersed myself in the media for a good part of my adult life, when I started writing this book, even I fought against the word. It seems too crass and self-serving to say, "Tom Peric', publicity expert." Remember my comment about journalists and the "I"

word. It's not my style to promote myself, but it is exactly what you must do. (Frankly, that's one of the reasons that I wrote this book. I also got tired of giving free advice.)

Using our restaurant example, don't fool yourself. Promoting your restaurant can be very tough, but promoting Chef Louie, an expert chef, is MUCH easier. Remember the rule: Journalists love stories about people and ideas. Who cares about another restaurant? But a story about this expert chef who's created five new recipes for Christmas. Now, there's a story. Here's what you need to know about being an expert and promoting your expertise.

You must promote your expertise if you want to gain maximum publicity. You can say you're an expert or have someone say it for you. This is the explicit approach. You can also imply it by what you do and have someone else assess you and infer (correctly) that you're an expert. The choice is yours. If you're uncomfortable sounding your own praises, and that's true for most of us, just let the media infer your expertise and then let them state it in their coverage either directly, by calling you an expert, or indirectly, by writing about the reasons that make you an expert. My final word on this is that if you call yourself an expert, you'll find that once the publicity bandwagon begins, it won't be necessary to promote yourself with the "E" word. Others, especially the media, will do it for you.

How recognized is your expertise? It's linked directly to how much effort you expend promoting your expertise. In short, how intense, how wise and how determined are you in – let's say it – self-promotion. The additional element is also, of course, how lucky you are.

How compelling is your expertise to the rest of the world? You might be the eighth-ranked checkers player in the United States, but most people probably won't care too much unless they play competitive checkers. However, if you have a sponsor who is a game company and they send you out to conduct simultaneous games at public venues, people will care because when they play you, it's their opportunity to beat the eighth-strongest checkers player in the United States. If they win, they can brag for years. (Imagine getting into the ring with the eighth-ranked boxer in the nation or playing across the net with the eighth-ranked tennis player in the United States.) It's not the overall size of the audience that matters for publicity. If it were, we would want the world's attention, wouldn't we? Realistically, it's the audience to whom you're promoting your expertise that matters. Yes, it could be the world, but it could also be a restaurant serving a radius of ten square blocks.

Tom's Tip: Here's my best tip for developing confidence as an expert. Start small, giving talks and lectures, writing short articles (all explained later in this book) until you develop more confidence publicly conveying your expertise both in conversation and by demonstrating it, if that's what is required. By feeling comfortable promoting your "expertise" on a smaller scale, you'll be ready when the big-time opportunities arrive.

The media anoints most experts. The media endorses many of our experts or at least gives them the "official" recognition the public accepts. The media is responsible for taking unrecognized experts and turning them into recognized experts. Now go out and promote yourself as an expert so that you become a *recognized* expert.

A few thoughts about experts and experience.

It takes a lot of time to get experience, and once you have it you ought to go on using it.
Benjamin M. Duggar, American botanist

An expert is a man who has made all the mistakes which can be made in a very narrow field.
Niels Bohr, physicist

[An expert is] somebody who is more than 50 miles from home, has no responsibility for implementing the advice he gives, and shows slides.
Edwin Meese 3rd, former White House counsel

Chapter 4

The Best Way To Get Publicity

Use The News

Getting free publicity starts with a very straightforward but important premise: The most effective way to get publicity is to use the media. It's one of the most pervasive influences in modern society. When you approach it correctly, you can gain access to the media for free. In doing so, you gain instant recognition from its audience who infer that because you are being interviewed, you must be an "expert." And when you earn that "expert" title, even if it's in the minds of readers, listeners and viewers, you've just won the first round in the publicity sweepstakes.

The first steps in gaining access to the media are to create news and to recognize what is news. Even professional journalists can disagree on what is news. One definition is that a story becomes news when "it is *relevant* to people's lives, *useful* to them or *interesting*." [Authors' emphasis noted in *The Art of Editing*, Sixth Edition]. Elements that affect news include the type of audience, impact, proximity of the story, timeliness, prominence of the subject, novelty and conflict. Probably the narrowest definition of the news (but one I've heard frequently) is that it is whatever the editor and reporter decide is news. This isn't too far from the truth.

An easier way to understand this concept of news for the layperson comes from Bob Rosner, one of the nation's top retention experts and the author of *Working Wounded* (www.workingwounded.com) and the *Boss's Survival Guide*. (Terrific books, I bought both but I'm prejudiced. He's my former college roommate.) According to Bob, hurricanes, murder, breakthrough technology and scientific discoveries are news. Everything else is "stuff." In short, some people and events become news by (almost) automatic acceptance from those who decide what appears in the media. Don't forget Bob's hurricanes and murder example. The rest of news coverage is far more subjective and made on a case-by-case basis, which dovetails nicely with my earlier observation that news is what the editor or reporter decide is news. Often media sift through the stuff, use it, and it becomes news.

The reality is that for most of us, what we have to offer the media is stuff and not news. **This doesn't mean you can't get media attention for your stuff.** It does mean that it's up to you to ensure that the media uses your "stuff" instead of someone else's. Tying all news or stuff together is the element of either time or space. Here's a good example of how to think of the media and its use of news (and stuff) in relation to time or space. If you have a tube shaped like a funnel, think of all the potential news and stuff sitting at the top part of the funnel with the larger opening. As you get down to the more narrow neck, less and less gets through. Indeed, only so much can get through at one time. The narrow neck of a funnel is time in broadcast media and the number of pages in print journalism. Broadcast can't "create" more minutes in an hour, and the number of pages a publication assigns to a magazine or newspaper is also finite. (Yes, the Internet will change this, but as long as traditional media continues to dominate, the situation remains the same.) Your job is to push your news or stuff through the funnel so that the media covers your story and not someone else's.

Think of a News Angle. How do you sell your stuff as news? You must dream, think and create a news angle that is interesting to the media you hope to influence. Here is a sampling of questions you might want to ask about yourself, your business or your organization.

Vive La Difference! What's really different or new about your business or organization? Beware of the word "unique" when pitching ideas to the media. I've read that some editors at *The New York Times* have actually outlawed the use of this word. Because, let's face it, very little is unique. However, that doesn't mean you're not doing something new, fresh or different with a slight twist. Search for that twist because it's all you need. A new restaurant is not news. Your son who's a legal partner and is only 11 years old is news. Telling the media you have "great" food is not news. Telling the media that you wake up every morning at 5 a.m. and buy produce at the local farmer's market for your restaurant is news.

Exciting Events Draw Crowds. Does your business or organization sponsor an event that you can publicize? Can you create an event that will draw the media? Opening a bar is not news, it's a media yawner. Publicizing the opening of your bar by handing out sobriety test kits to the first 1,000 patrons is news. Owning a bedding company and carrying a new line of mattresses is boring. Who cares? Donating four beds to your local sleep clinic at the university is news.

Make A Top 10 List And Count The Ways. This is so easy, it's unbelievable that more people don't do it. Arbitrarily create your own top 10 list and update it periodically (quarterly, biannually or annually). It can also be a top 100 or the best of . . . etc.) The best-known example of this is Mr. Blackwell (What is his first name?), who issues his "Hollywood's worst-dressed actresses" list, which seems to crop up during Academy Awards time. Everyone listens to this guy's pronouncements via the media all over the world after the Oscar ceremony. (I just wonder what he does the rest of the time. I know this: If it wasn't working for him, he wouldn't do it.) The 10 Best Anything always gets play. Just remember to keep it up for the long haul so that you really reap the benefits. That means, don't begin it one year and then drop it.

Play Social Scientist. Issue a research study. Now this is slightly tricky but a great technique. Research doesn't mean it must pass the standards for peer review in the *Journal of the American Medical Association*. Even a small, basic study that might not pass statistical or scientific scrutiny CAN pass the media's inspection. Have you or could you conduct some fresh or new research that would gain press attention? Can you issue a press release, for example, that indicates people have new needs when it comes to joining a health club? People no longer go to the gym as a substitute for a singles bar, nor do they exercise because they want bigger muscles. After conducting a survey of more than 100 members, you've discovered that most people go to the gym because they're afraid of dying and think that exercise might keep them on this planet just a little longer. I can see the headline. Fear of Dying Drives People to Gym. (Or something like that.) When I wrote this, I was being slightly tongue-in-cheek, but as I think about it, I'd go with this "research" if my survey really indicated data along those lines. Here's the great thing about conducting your own research or study. First, you really might get some wild results (like my example) that you never thought about. Secondly, it really is an original study even though it might be unscientific. (Aren't "true" scientific studies flawed sometimes?) Third, **NEVER** lie to the media. Say I conducted a survey of 100 people and asked these questions. Based on the answers, this is the result of the survey. The fact that your survey touches upon an issue that has universal interest is your good fortune.

Here's a real-life example. A friend of mine wanted to penetrate a particular industry. He helps business people create Web sites. I told him to study 20 or so web sites (of small, medium and large companies) and write an article about what he thought they did well and what they did poorly. Then I told him to issue his results – a study – to the local trade press. No one else had done this, or at least no one had conducted similar research and issued a press release. How extensive was the study? About 20 pages. He's now an "expert" on Web design in that industry. For this type of research, you don't have to stand up to scientific analysis. You do have to stand up to common sense and thoroughness.

Everyone Loves A Winner. Contests and awards are shortcuts to media attention. A contest should be fun and interesting. You boost the attention-grabbing value if it helps a worthy cause or has terrific or unusual prizes. Awards should be meaningful because the recipient really did something. (See Chapter 17 for more details.)

Timing Is (Almost) Everything. It really is. Can you take whatever you want to publicize and tie it to a trend, anniversary, holiday or current event? Why do you think the media interviews Pearl Harbor vets every Dec. 7th? This is the 100th anniversary of the invention of air conditioning. If you have a heat wave and you're in the air conditioning business . . . well, I hope you get the message. For specifics about how to almost "automatically" find a hook for your product or service with timing, see Chapter 15 on Wacky Days.

I'm Right And You're Wrong. Going against the tide can be fun IF you don't mind the criticism. Sending out a press release where you challenge popular opinion will get you attention. If you're a rope manufacturer and believe that public hangings should come back into vogue (not my opinion), try sending a press release and a noose to the top editors in the country and your local TV station. I'll bet you get publicity. (I must add that the type of publicity you get might NOT be the kind you are seeking.) If you're shy and dislike controversy, taking a contrarian view probably won't fit your style. If you're Churchillian in your approach and you love the slash and stab of verbal swordsmanship, then this could be your métier. My only advice is that if you choose to take a contrarian position, be sure you're firmly rooted with defensible facts, in your camp. You might need more than "I just feel that way." The reasoning is clear-cut. If the media pays attention to your views the first time and realizes that you're nothing more than an opinionated blowhard, you might not get a second opportunity. I confess that I'm personally partial to contrarians, maybe because they wring some reaction out of me.

Did You Hear The Joke About . . . ? Using humor to gain publicity is great, but this is one of the most difficult tactics to carry out. What's funny to one person is an insult to another. In our politically correct climate, it's even tougher. That's why when it does work, the effects can be far-reaching. If you're an editorial consultant and, tongue-in-cheek, created a list of the 10 most intelligent comments made by politicians, then went on to show how shallow those comments are – and by inference, the politicians who uttered them – this could work. Just be careful if your target is NOT a public figure. It's extremely difficult for a public person to win a libel suit, but everyone wants to sue these days. Of course, you could take the attitude, " . . . if they can't take a joke."

When you're having a dull day (no ideas) going through this list as you daydream about your next pitch to the media, relax for a few minutes and see if you can create something just a little bit different. It'll be worth the effort, and by trying various angles, you'll fight the boredom of cranking out the "same old stories." And what you might find instead is a fresh twist to an old idea. Someone has done it before, and someone will do it again. Just try to be the person who occasionally discovers the twist.

Chapter 5

Contacting The Media

Who Are Those News People?

The starting point for every publicity campaign begins with the media you want to influence. You must discover and decide who you want to inform or contact in the media. The appraisal must be realistic. Sure, we all want to be on the front page of *The New York Times* or *The Wall Street Journal*, but it's not particularly realistic unless you have a story worthy of national attention. (Do you want a guarantee for national media attention? Go out and commit some horrific crime. I don't suggest or condone this approach, but you will get media coverage.) You might decide that the neighborhood newspaper is the only publication that interests you. Or it might be a friend's newsletter. It could be *Variety* magazine, the *Philadelphia Enquirer*. Or ABC's *Nightline* news show.

It's really a bit like sales. You ask, "Who do I want to know about my product or service?" Then you ask, "How do those people receive their information?" If you have a local bike shop and you're not on the Internet, your local weekly and daily newspapers and a few community newspapers in your county might encompass your media list. If you're a manufacturer of lawn equipment, it might include trade magazines for the industry and consumer magazines that deal with lawn care. When you understand and decide who you want to influence and what media you want to approach, then you can go about influencing the media outlets you've chosen. How do you find this media? Here's where to look.

Local and Regional Press Sources:

Try your local reference library and ask them if there is a local media directory.

Yellow Pages. Look under Newspapers, News Publications, Newsletters, Radio Stations and Broadcasting Companies, and Television Stations and Broadcasting Companies. You can create your own list, and it's free. Trying the library and telephone book might seem low-tech in this Internet age, but if you're a small, strictly local business, it's all you need. Also, add any publications that you see when traveling through your community. I see free publications at my supermarket, gym and various restaurants that I frequent. Combing the telephone list, your library sources and your travel list should be sufficient for small, local media campaigns. And it costs nothing.

Call your local newspaper and ask if there is a press club in the area. If there is, call the press club and ask them if they have a directory. You might have to pay for this directory, but it can be quite useful. For example, locally, we have the New Jersey Press Association (www.njpa.org). For $25 you receive a complete listing of newspapers throughout the state. (Frankly, I don't know whether you get broadcast media, but this is still a cheap, effective directory.)

For my "local" clients in the Delaware Valley, I use the *Greater Philadelphia Media Guide*. This annual publication costs about $70 from Balset Co., P.O. Box 283, West Point, PA 19486, (215) 699-9277 www.philamediaguide.com. This guide has everything, including radio and television programs, programming focus, newspapers, etc. They update it annually.

National Press Sources

There are national companies that provide media directories, but these can be very expensive. They include:

- Burrelle's
  75 E. Northfield Rd.
  Livingston, NJ 07039
  800-631-1160 (www.Burrelles.com)

- Bacon's Media Directories
  322 S. Michigan Ave.
  Chicago, IL 60604,
  800-753-6675 (www.bacons.com)

Both of these companies publish a series of voluminous media directories, including newspaper, magazine, radio and TV. They are expensive but available in major libraries.

- I use *The News Media Yellow Book*. Expensive. About $325 per book, and they have a number of directories, which they issue quarterly. Contact: Leadership Directories, 1301 Pennsylvania Avenue. N.W., Washington, D.C. 20004 (202) 347-7757; fax (202) 628-3430 (www.leadershipdirectories.com)
- I also use *Publicity Blitz* by Bradley Communications Corp., 135 East Plumstead Ave., P.O. Box 1206, Landsdowne PA 19050-8206 (610) 259-0707; Fax (610) 284-3704. Reasonably priced at about $295. (I understand they've discontinued this directory. Pity, because it was certainly affordable. They have a few left over at discount prices and might be worth contacting. After all, while employees leave frequently, the address for most newspapers, radio and TV stations change incrementally.)
- For a great list of top radio stations, see Alex Carroll in Chapter 24.

A word about directories. The way directories make money after you've bought one is by claiming that they update their directories every year. It's true that personnel change in the media is rampant. Directory companies would also argue that sending a press release to a specific person has a stronger impact than sending it strictly by title. This is probably true, though I've never seen a study to prove it. For most publicity campaigns, it really doesn't matter. First, you really don't know if the person on your list is at that media outlet, because by the time you have the directory (or even the "update"), things could have changed. Again. Second, I've been in a number of newsrooms and plenty of editorial offices, and, believe me, as long as they think it's for them – name or title – they'll open it. It's the information inside that matters, not what's on the outside of the envelope. I mention this because if you're a small-business owner or a not-for-profit, you could go broke buying new directories. Let's be blunt. How many daily newspapers, radio stations and television stations "close" or shut their doors every year? (Magazines are another issue, if you'll excuse the pun.) For pros in the business, buying a directory every year might make sense. For others, a good directory every 2 – 3 years should be just fine. What really matters is how you maintain your important primary list, which I'll explain later.

Tom's Tip: When buying a directory, try to buy one that is on a CD-Rom or that you can download from the Internet. The reason is straightforward. You can manipulate the information as you see fit. For example, if you need all the radio stations in Delaware, it takes a minute to draw them up on your screen. You can even focus the campaign to a specific zip code. Finally, with an electronic version of your media list, you can easily and quickly create mailing labels.

Warning: If you buy a media list that you're going to import into your computer, be sure that you have the software to "run" or manipulate the information. Some directories require a database, such as Microsoft's Access, which in all likelihood was not a standard feature when you bought your computer. Buying it separately could cost about $300, adding another cost to what you just shelled out for the media directory. For micro-businesses or not-for-profits, it might be a sour revelation.

Important: Also be aware that all companies which produce media directories have migrated to the Internet. You pay a fee, then have access for a certain period. Thus you won't be able to use your "old" directory.

The Primary List. The secret to maintaining your primary or most important list is uncomplicated. If you need a list that goes beyond the local list I've already mentioned, you should do this.

Step 1: Create or buy the media list that interests you. (Remember that if you BUY the list, you can usually use it ONLY once.) Let me explain a distinction. If you buy a media database in hard copy, you hold a volume in your hand and use it as often as you want. If you buy a database and access it via the Internet, you can use it an unlimited number of times for the duration of your subscription (usually a year). But some companies also sell lists of media contacts so that you can send your target audience a press release. You go to *Bacon's*, for example, and buy a list of all the magazines they have in their database that deal with manufacturing. I did this as a real test and came up with 200 magazines. I can now buy the names of magazines (and the names of editors as well) and download the information into my computer, make mailing labels from the information and send them a press release. Purchases like this usually involve the right to use the list one time (less expensive) OR as often as I wish during a specified period (more expensive). Back to my warning. If you buy the list for one-time use, you cannot use it a second time. How do they know? They "seed" the list with dummy names who have the responsibility of reporting misuse of the list. Using a list more frequently than your agreement is unethical and possibly illegal; so don't do it.

Step 2: Create a 3-tier approach for press releases, calls, etc. That simply means that your most important media is the A-list; the second most important is the B-list; and the C-list is your least important. Now, if you're mailing a press release, the entire list should get the release.

Step 3: You should restrict efforts to calling or meeting with editors only if they're on your A-list and possibly the B-list (unless you have nothing better to do). You simply won't have time to follow up on everything. (Only in rare cases and with a small list have I ever bothered to approach the C-list).

Tom's Tip: The exception to this rule is that if a member of your B or C list contacts you and seems interested in what you do, give this person or outlet all the attention they want. Also, I would promote them to the A-list even though they might not fit the criteria you established for it. Their interest in you and the possibility that they will write or broadcast your story should overcome any reluctance you might have about placing them on the A-list. The key is to take this type of contact and remain on friendly terms with them for future stories. I'll always take an easy placement on a story even if it's a C-list media outlet, especially when I find a friendly, interested journalist.

Chapter 6

The Timing Issue

Timing & Issues = Opportunity

"I hear you knocking . . ."

When I sit down with a potential client, they naturally assess me based on my background, current client list, past successes and the indefinable, "Can I work with this guy?" They also want to know what background, experience and knowledge I have and whether it fits with their publicity and public relations goals. These are all legitimate questions that you should always ask a person involved in the publicity business like me. Then I usually tell them about something else that I bring to the table which they seldom think about.

When someone hires me for publicity and public relations services, I offer what I term as my "scouting service." I've noticed that my clients seem momentarily puzzled when I mention it. When I explain how it works, they always respond with a predictable, "Ah, ha."

In my early days of probing for publicity on behalf of my clients, I had the owner of a funeral home as a client. Now, that's a challenge. Trying to drum up publicity for a funeral home owner could be deadly. In fact, when I went on to larger clients, I could say without equivocation that this client will never receive the publicity that he gained when we worked together. He appeared in a major city magazine touting his efforts in his neighborhood. His picture and quotes appeared in one of the nation's largest slick, four-color magazines aimed at small businesses. His two neighborhood newspapers ran favorable stories about him after a fire destroyed part of his business. The local newspaper, a huge daily, published a major feature using him as a source (with a photo) on how to overcome hardships in business.

The point of this recitation is that when a client comes aboard with me, I think about them all the time. I had the funeral home owner on my mind every day. That's why he got such incredible results. If you're a lawyer and you're my client, I'm constantly thinking of ways to insert you into the media mix. Anything that I hear, read, think about, see or even smell, if it has a legal connection to your specialty, I'm wondering how I can introduce you and your firm or organization into the news. This is the way you must think if you intend to pursue publicity on a long-term basis. The difficulty here, of course, is making the mental switch (and finding the necessary time) from running your business or organization to focusing on how to connect with a newsworthy event or opportunity that translates into publicity for you.

Let's use a few examples. Several weeks after the terrible attack on the World Trade Center there happens to be a growing interest, according to the media, in people purchasing firearms and gas masks. If you're in the firearms business, this screams for a time to write an information tip sheet, idea tip sheet, newsletter or even just a note to a journalist suggesting they write a piece about how to decide: 1) whether you should own a firearm; 2) which firearm is "right" for you if you decide to buy; 3) and most important, how to safely store your firearm in a home with small children. This is not taking advantage of a horrific event that affected all of us. This is about sharing your expertise so that people, should they decide to purchase a firearm, can make an informed, rational decision. With your perspective, you just might prevent some people from purchasing a gun based on raw emotion and a slick-talking salesman (who might want to sell a firearm with the largest markup) rather than a decision which rests on your needs, physical capability, personal style and family issues. **Keep in mind when the media needs information or are searching for an expert, they will find someone, whether or not it's you. You have to decide if you want to be a candidate in their search.**

In a less intense example, every winter, first-time skiers take to the slopes. After spending a small fortune on this new adventure, including lift tickets and new or rented skis, everyone troops up to the top of the mountain (OK, maybe a hill) and takes their plunge. Some will suffer injury, even more will have aches and pains, and a few will suffer serious harm.

If you are a personal fitness trainer, wouldn't it make sense to offer a tip sheet about the five exercises you can begin to perform in October so that when you first take to the slopes, the transition to a new form of exercise will be less traumatic? Now I don't know what those five exercises might be, but I'm sure a personal trainer would know, especially if he skis.

In both examples, it's a matter of timing. The only difference is the predictability factor. In one case, you can't predict that an event will occur (an act of terrorism and the aftershocks); in the other case, you know that an event is coming (a change in season).

But being on the alert or scouting for opportunity is a mind-set that you must develop for your business or not-for-profit if you want to tap into free exposure. With all due modesty, I can say that most of my clients love it when they get that unexpected call from me suggesting we do something – usually with some urgency – to tap into an opportunity that I've discovered. Speed is the key, especially when you find yourself assessing a sudden or unexpected event in an area in which you are familiar. You must present your idea **quickly** to the media while the event is fresh in everyone's mind. You must respond as quickly as possible with a tip sheet, letter to the editor, op-ed piece, before the momentary interest passes. If an event occurs and you feel that your background gives you some expertise that you would like to share through a letter to the editor, that's great. Don't waste time writing the letter if it's more than a week or 10 days after the event. In most cases, the editor will consider your comments to be "old news." (Unless it's a running story, which means it continues to unfold over days, weeks and even months.) Because most of you operate or work for businesses and organizations, it might be difficult to drop what you're doing and take advantage of the situation. You will have to discipline yourself to do so and do it quickly or hire someone who can. Otherwise, the opportunity will slip through your fingers.

Tom's Tip: When I think of this entire timing issue, I see several points to follow. Because most of you lack a paid publicity person like me to conduct the scouting, you'll have to do it. The secret is to respond immediately. *Don't overthink it.* That means, if you spot an event that cries for an Op-Ed piece, don't keep delaying until the passage of time gives the story a stale odor. Do this:

Step 1: Decide to do something.

Step 2: Figure out what is the best approach (you have my book in your hand).

Step 3: Decide who will do it: you, an employee or someone hired for the assignment.

Step 4: Begin. If you're performing the task, take the evening off and write that Op-Ed piece (don't forget to have someone edit your work). If your employee or the publicity person you hired is responsible, give them a firm deadline. Then you're done, and you should have reasonable expectations for free publicity.

What makes timing so exquisitely attractive is that it's part of everyday living. It only takes you to recognize how the timing of events can further your publicity aims.

Chapter 7

The Press Release

Transforming The Publicity Draft Horse Into A Racehorse

Write A Press Release. You've got your news angle. You've figured out what idea you want to sell (or pitch, as they say in PR) to the media. Now write a press release about it. A press release is a brief document, usually one to two pages in length, which explains why the media should cover you, your event, product, service or business. The press release is still the workhorse of the publicity business, especially for people with no contacts in the media who can't just pick up the phone, call a reporter and say, "I've got a great story. You should cover it."

Writing a press release in an attempt at getting publicity is as basic as brushing your teeth in the morning. While there isn't much difference between toothpastes (regardless of the hype), press releases are NOT all created equal. In order to have the media pick up (use) your release, it's going to have to stand out from the crowd. Here's a fact that will make you weep. Major newspapers receive hundreds, if not thousands, of press releases every day. Even the business desk of a small (less than 50,000 circulation), daily newspaper probably receives a dozen press releases each day. National magazines receive upwards of a thousand or more press releases each month. What that means is you must cut through the avalanche so that editors pay attention to your press release. Here's how.

Secrets of a Successful Press Release

- **Secret 1: Write a great headline.** A great headline is one that has a news angle. It's the grabber. This might be the single most important advice that I can share. If you don't get the editor to pay attention to the headline, you've probably wasted the precious few seconds you have to get his attention, thereby killing any chance of the editor using your press release.
- **The Benefit, Please!** Get to the heart of it. Tell the reader – immediately – what's in it for them. For example, "Lure manufacturer says new product will help you catch twice as many bass as any other product." It's a long title, but if you're a bass fisherman, you'll probably continue to read to the next paragraph.
- **Secret 2: Provide the Who, What, When, Where and Why (or How) in the first paragraph.** If you wrote a good headline, you must now fulfill your promise of giving more information by making it as compelling as you can. We call this the lead (or lede, as many journalists spell it). It is usually the first paragraph in a story or press release. Sometimes the lead is only a single sentence. People often assume that because I've spent so much time in the writing business, I would have all kinds of quotes, anecdotes and word-related trivia around my desk and decorating my walls. I don't. I keep one quote pasted on my wall, and it probably gives the best advice I've ever read (or heard) when it comes to discussing how to write the lead (or opening paragraph) and hold the reader's attention. **"Always grab the reader by the throat in the first paragraph, sink your thumbs into his windpipe in the second, and hold him against the wall until the tag line."** – Paul O'Neil, 20th-century American writer.

Now you know as much about writing a lead as I do. One marketing expert suggests you write at least 50 headlines and 10 leads before settling on the best one. Do as many as you feel are necessary before staleness sets in. If you can't decide between your two or three top choices and your gut isn't talking to you, ask three people whose judgment you trust. If they all pick the same one, you've got a winner.

- **Secret 3: Quote somebody.** Use a quote in your second paragraph. Be sure that your quote, colorful whenever possible, supports a reason behind the press release. Just like press releases, all quotes do NOT have the same impact. Quote the most impressive person you can. This might be an industry leader or simply Joe Smith, bass fisherman for 40 years. Obtaining a quote from an expert or a celebrity gives your press release a verbal blessing that it might otherwise lack. The "real" secret here is not to use made-up, artificial-sounding, pompous, say-nothing sentences which give the reader no new information and only serve to boost the speaker's ego. I have a tendency to use everyday language because it's real. Believe me, I can usually tell when I see a manufactured quote in a press release. Most editors can, too. It doesn't mean they won't use the press release, but it does mean that the release is more suspect. Here's an example: "American Independent Toilet (AIT) profits had record sales last year because our highly talented management team incorporated a market-driven analysis and super sales techniques combined with an almost flawless leadership style that combined for a superb performance in a shifting economy," said Joe Smith, company president.

Whew, what is that, and do I care? It sounds like some public relations person wrote it hoping to boost the ego of this executive windbag. (The reason for many of these say-nothing, pompous quotes written by PR people is because the executive wants to sound important or the PR person believes that supposition.) Now here's how the president should say it: "American Independent Toilet (AIT) profits had record sales last year because we identified a new market niche and hammered it with four new salespeople," said Joe Smith, company president. "We also keep a lid on expenses and ruthlessly cut the fat, reducing operating costs by 5 percent without letting go of one employee or touching any employee benefits. We have a secret. Everyone talks about teamwork. We actually practice it." Sure, the second quote is longer, but so what? Isn't it better because it's more believable and readable? Notice the second quote uses shorter sentences. Here's something to consider. The first quote, pompous as it was, only used 44 words. The second quote, which was real, used 68 words. Why does the first one seem longer? Because it says nothing and it's boring.

Tom's Tip: Use short sentences when writing quotes. The longer the sentence, the less likely an editor will use it, especially if it's meaningless. Shorter sentences raise the odds of the editor using your quote, providing it says something relevant to the story.

Secret 4: Expand on the information in the previous paragraphs. This is where you flesh out the information you've already shared. You can pull in another quote, quote yourself for a change, and add biographical data or historical information. It's also a great place to add a comparison. This is where you want to put your information in context for the editor.

Secret 5: Close the deal. Here's where you end with the bottom line: How can people reach you or buy your product or service? Be sure that you use contact information and details such as name, price, address, telephone, fax and e-mail address. If you're "selling" something, NEVER send a press release out without this paragraph. Yes, my journalist friends will say, "we'll just cut that portion out." The truth is that sometimes part of it will make it into the media and sometimes ALL of it will appear. Let the editor make the choice, just be sure that you give it to him.

Can writing an effective press release really make that much of a difference? My buddy and one of my two personal advertising gurus, Adams Hudson, turned his press release over to me (after all, I'm the publicity guru, according to Adams) for a quick look. I rewrote 11 different versions before I felt satisfied with the final one. Keep a couple of things in mind:

- His original press release probably would have worked. It just wouldn't have worked as well as the one I completed.
- There really were 11 drafts. In the Appendix, I show you the third and the final draft. A draft doesn't mean there was a complete rewrite. I might have only changed a few words or added several sentences. However, each time I was done, I'd find something new. (This answers that question about, "Can you just knock out a press release in 30 minutes?" or the other question: "You want how much for a press release?") You see, writing a press release that works is work.
- Is my release perfect? No. I'm sure you could still make some improvements. But (blushing) it's the results that matter.

Here's what Adams said: "I consider myself a pretty good copywriter but had gotten nowhere with my press releases. After getting your input on rewriting mine, I was amazed at the simplicity and clarity you presented.

"After I sent out my 'improved' press release, I was shocked to find that – to date – it has been printed in 11 different publications, resulting in a pile of requests and phone calls. I cannot thank you enough." (Muffled applause.) Before I take all the credit, the first release that Adams wrote was decent – after all, he does know advertising. I was quite certain that I better understood the minds of the editors who would look at it. Also, and this is important, Adams really HAD something of value to offer. **No matter how much he and I crafted a terrifically worded press release, it would have sunk like the Titanic had the reason for the release not merited attention.**

Tom's Tip: Before you begin writing your press release, ask and answer two important questions: Why should I care, and why should I care now? Because subconsciously, that's what the editor will be asking on behalf of his readers. No one cares what you think or why you think it's important. It must matter to the audience of the press release, and the timeliness of the release gives it an urgency it might not otherwise have.

Tom's Tip: How to find someone to write your press release. Let's say you have no one who can write a press release in your organization (including you). You can choose to forego sending out press releases, but that's probably a mistake. You can call me, but I'm expensive. Call your local weekly or daily newspaper. Ask for the editor or managing editor and say you would like to hire a writer for a free-lance writing assignment. If they ask what kind of assignment, just say you need someone to write a press release. I favor local weekly newspaper writers because their pay is so meager and yet many are skillful. Ask the writer what he charges, and if you're comfortable with the fee, tell him what you need. I would suspect that you could get a basic press release written for $200 to $400 dollars. You've just solved your writing problem. (Don't forget: When you have a completed press release, be sure to submit it to the publication for which your writer works IF it's an appropriate media outlet.)

I will consider it personal thanks from you the reader if you write a successful press release. The ONLY judgment of that is if the media uses it. Don't forget, come up with a good news angle for your business, write a good, clean, press release, answer the two questions you must address, follow the format I've suggested and then mail (fax or e-mail) it to the "right" media list. Then sit back and have a mint julep because you'll feel terrific when someone in the media "picks up" (publishes) your press release. It feels great.

Chapter 8

Write Makes It Right

And Turns You Into An Expert

The quickest and best way to being a recognized expert is to write a book. Period. By becoming an author, you also become a *recognized* expert, and naturally the media is more likely to either write about you or turn to you as a source when writing about your area or specialty. That's the easy part, recognizing the potent power of the written word (on paper and electronically) and its immediate ability to confer the title of "expert" on someone.

Any time you're promoting yourself to your peers or potential customers, but especially to the media, the accomplishment of being an author is really a stamp of approval regarding your expertise. A book demonstrates that you know so much about your topic and that you're so thoughtful about the subject that you sat down, mulled it over and then wrote it all down. You really have a body of knowledge, and here you are proving it.

I could go on and on, but you probably get the point. It still amazes me how the heft of a book continues to make a powerful and positive impression on a person. It really confirms your status as an expert, which you can (literally) take with you. The sheer existence of your book allows you to promote yourself without the trappings of a carnival barker. It makes you more authentic. I suspect that we have such respect for book authors because we know either from experience or intuitively how difficult it is to actually finish a book. (I'll have more to say about this shortly.) Indeed, the better known you wish to become, the more mandatory it becomes to write large, which for most people means writing a book. The goal of writing a book might present you with a problem that could be insurmountable.

Tom's Tip: Here's an undemanding suggestion and a solution to your potential problem. Read this chapter at least once. If a book isn't for you – and frankly, it isn't for many people – go on to the other chapters on gaining publicity. You have many choices. By reading through once, you'll know what you must confront and, thankfully, not have to face. Of course, something else might happen. You'll find that writing a book is not nearly as difficult as you imagined or as intimidating as some people claim. (It really isn't.) Now I want to dispel one major myth about writing a book here, now and forever. Later in this chapter I'll share with you the ONLY real law you'll have to follow if you wish to write a book. Everything else is secondary.

Destroying A Myth. If you buy into the idea that you need a book for raising your visibility – and that's a good notion – but you're convinced that you can't write a book because of various obstacles, put your doubts aside for the moment. Let me destroy this myth once and for all. Most people reject the idea of writing a book for the usual reasons: You're not a *writer*, you question your grasp of grammar, you're afraid that you won't sound intelligent enough or you don't have anything new to write about. Banish these ideas. Immediately. Here's the clear, unvarnished truth. We're not talking about writing literature (or fiction, for that matter), and we're not talking about writing a great book that will bring tears, terror or contemplation to your audience. You don't have to emotionally touch your readers. You don't have to entertain your readers (unless that's your goal). Lastly, we're not discussing writing a bestseller.

So what **must** you do? **All you have to do is simply inform your readers in a style that's readable.**

Nothing more. What we are talking about is putting together a few reasonable ideas, expressed in simple, clean English, one page after another until you have no more to say.

If you can create a reasonable outline and you can express yourself with simple, "nickel" words and string together these words so they express a coherent sentence, you can become an author and write a book. That means you've gotten together enough of these pages so that, at some point, you have placed enough information that appears on the printed page and which you've placed between two covers. Then you bind the pages together and call it a book.

Is it really that simple? It really is, though the physical task of finishing a book is not a trifle, and the discipline of completing the writing journey is probably the largest stumbling block that most people confront. I've heard every cliché you can think of when it comes to writing and comparing it with a long journey, climbing a mountain, running a marathon. This is true, but only to a degree. After all, most mountains are not the height of Mt. Everest. Indeed, some mountains are only big hills. The same applies to the effort involved in writing a book. If a characteristic of your personality requires you to look for immediate gratification, writing a book might not be the vehicle that you should use for your publicity campaign.

But if you want to give it a shot, it's this easy:

Tom's Tip: The 100 Percent Guaranteed Way To Write Your Book With A Little Bit of Effort and Commitment.

Book Writing Step 1: Pick a working title for your book. This means a sentence or phrase.

Book Writing Step 2: Create an outline by writing a one-sentence headline for each chapter. If you really want to go wild, write a subhead or second sentence to support or more clearly explain the chapter title.

Book Writing Step 3: Write whatever you know about each chapter until you have said everything you want to say.

Book Writing Step 4: When you're done writing each chapter, go back and rewrite everything you've done ONE time. In other words, take another look at everything you wrote. Edit yourself.

Book Writing Step 5: Show your book to NO MORE THAN FIVE PEOPLE WHOSE OPINION YOU VALUE AND WHO WOULD UNDERSTAND THE USEFULNESS OF WHAT YOU WROTE. Do NOT show it to more than five people (two to three is just fine) because there's no end to the comments or suggestions you'll get. It's your book, not a book by committee.

Book Writing Step 6: Make any changes that you wish to accept from the people who gave you comments.

Book Writing Step 7: When writing a book, there is one little, dirty secret that most people never know or don't think about. The editor can often make, break or save a book. Give your book to a professional editor. **I can't stress this enough.** It must be someone who has strong editing skills and experience in editing. Have the person edit you for content and grammar, etc. You can reject your editor's comments about content if they don't know your area of expertise, but don't dismiss his comments if they deal with clarity, word meaning, etc. Get the best editor you can find and afford. A good editor will always make you appear to be a much better writer than you actually are. God knows, it's certainly true in my case. I've had the same editor for more than a decade and I'd find it very difficult to live without him. My casual topics or less important articles or first drafts often go to my sister, who's a terrific proofreader even though she doesn't do it professionally. Then it goes to my editor for the last look. When someone compliments me on my writing and editing skills, they both deserve a great deal of the praise.

How do you find a good editor? I honestly can't think of a sure-fire way other than to ask around. What's important here is not that someone is or was a writer but rather that they served as an editor of a publication. You want a person who actually handled writers' copy with the intent of making it more readable by viewing it with an eye toward rules of grammar, logic, thoroughness and accurate reporting. Above all, an editor must ensure the copy is clear to the audience it targets. Here are a few suggestions for finding an editor:

- Call your local press club or daily or weekly newspaper and ask if they have a copy editor who takes on freelance assignments. A copy editor is a person who checks what someone writes for grammar, usage and style.
- Call the local English department of a college or university IF you write for an academic audience. (I hope academics will forgive me but while their writing is often grammatically correct, it usually reads with a recognizable academic jargon and style. Translation? Academic prose is English that's boring and heavy going.)
- Look at a copy of your favorite local or national magazine and call the editor or managing editor and ask if they have someone who is interested in editing.
- Give them a test. Take something you've written and give it to your two or three best candidates. That will be the final test. Keep in mind that reliability, meeting deadlines and a comfortable relationship are almost as important as pure editing skills. (Fortunately, my editors get A's in all departments.)
- Hold on to a good editor and don't let him go away. They are invaluable to every good writer. If you use an editor infrequently, stay in touch. You never know when you might need his skills.

- How did I meet my editor? He edited copy for a magazine to which I contributed business stories. When I wrote a mini-book, I was smart enough to know that I needed an editor. I asked him, and he did a fine job. I stayed in touch and whenever I had articles that needed editing, I usually turned to him. I've never been disappointed, and that's why I urge people to keep good editors when they find them.

Now comes the caveat that you're expecting. **Caveat.** Unless you're a superb and talented writer, I want to repeat the importance of Steps 4 and 7. Be prepared to rewrite what you've written at least once or twice. (Do not rewrite more than twice or you simply might never finish the book. There are uncounted numbers of manuscripts that litter the writing landscape which only need "just a touch-up" or one more draft before they're ready. Don't fall into the analysis - paralysis trap.)

I remember James Michener, who sold millions of books, once saying that he wasn't a very good writer but that he was a pretty good rewriter. Little secret: That's true of most writers. You must also know when to stop.

I hate to surprise you, but that's all there is to it, if you really know the topic about which you're writing. This book started out exactly in the manner I've described. Sure, just like adjusting to a new girlfriend or boyfriend, you make some changes along the way, add elements and reduce or eliminate others, but now you know the secret for writing nonfiction.

But I Just DON'T Want To Write The Damn Thing. There's another way to become a writer without really writing anything. You can hire someone to ghostwrite the book for you. This is the ideal approach if you're determined to establish your expertise and recognize the need for a book without actually "writing" one. This means you "hire out" your ideas, giving the information to a professional who writes it while you take credit as the author. You would be stunned at how many people have done this. You can dictate your ideas or simply put them down in whatever style you wish. A good writer will be able to turn out a manuscript that is polished, informative and comprehensive within your timeframe. The writer also will make you appear to be a far better writer than you probably are, but that's OK. Don't lose a great deal of sleep over this issue. If you're 30, you're probably NOT going to improve your skills as a professional writer without enormous effort. Who has the time? You're involved in promoting your business or organization, not honing your writing skills. Simply use the shortcuts that are available. If I have a plumbing problem, I can try fixing it on my own or I can call the plumber. I don't have insomnia over the fact that my skills simply don't include plumbing. Why should you feel any different about writing?

Here's what's great about writing a book. Even if you're a lousy expert, dead wrong about the topic and clueless about developments in your field, a book still makes you an expert. The great part about writing a book is that no one contradicts you, unless you choose to allow this to happen in your book. (This does happen in book reviews if you're lucky enough to have someone review your book.) It's a great way to tell a one-sided story, though I would suggest that if you're too far off base and your readers suspect this, you will begin to lose credibility, especially with people who might have an impact on your book sales. I want to turn to the issue about how to publish your book and offer a few tips about how to market yourself with a book. Because that's what it's all about.

Publish, Perish Or Profit? Before you're done with your book, you need to have a sense about which way to publish it: Do you self-publish or approach a mainstream publisher? Here's the short answer.

All things being equal for most people, I'd say go with a publisher. However, because all things are not equal, therefore my advice to most of you is that you should, initially, publish your own book.

When you go to a publisher, you get your idea accepted, write the book, complete any rewriting or shortcomings the editor at the publishing house notices and then hand the book back to the publisher, who actually creates the book and markets it. You'll probably get about 10 to 15 percent commission on each copy sold. Actually, if you have an agent, he'll get the commission check and deduct his 10 to 15 percent for acting as your agent. You get the rest. The publisher will have a great deal to say about the approach, nature and tone of your book. Why shouldn't he? It's the publisher's money that is at risk, not yours. He'll have a firm deadline in mind. That means that you're on the publisher's publishing list, which usually occurs in the fall or spring every year. It also means that once the book is "done," you'll probably wait another three months to a year before you actually see it. Oh, yes. What about publicity for your book and what about your advance, future sales, bookstores, etc? Here's the reality: 1) You'll probably get between $5,000 and $10,000 in advance for your book (AGAINST your commissions, of course); 2) You'll have minimal to zero publicity budget for your book; 3) About 5,000 to 10,000 books will be printed, and they'll disappear from bookstores in 30 to 90 days, then get sent back to the publisher for a credit; 4) Chances are that there won't be a second printing run for your book. Pretty grim, isn't it? Still want to be an expert? Still want a major publishing house to publish your book? It's extremely difficult to become a published author, and it's even more difficult to make any real money doing it, despite what you've read about those large advances to famous authors. (It's natural to read about the millions of books that John Grisham sells and automatically start multiplying his royalties in your head.) Visit a Borders, Barnes & Noble or even your local independently owned bookstore. (That's my plug for independent bookstores. Support them.) Go to the section where your book would fit on the shelf. Those books are the competition. Having said all of this, the upside is that you

ARE swinging for the fences with a book, which means you could create a bestseller that will earn tons of money and a quick ticket on the radio-TV guest show appearance circuit. It's just that the odds are so against you. The biggest question the publisher has other than will the book sell (which means, is the idea marketable?) is whether you'll deliver the book. That means the publisher is wondering whether you'll really write the entire book and whether or not you'll deliver it on time. Because most publishers release books only a few times each year to meet their catalog schedule for new releases, the deadline becomes important. Here's a quick tip that might help. A plethora of books cover the subject of how to become a published author, and I'm not going to cover this vast topic here. The Appendix has a list of books that I recommend.

Tom's Tip: Writers, especially those who don't really write a great deal, and even more especially would-be book writers, love to read about the writing techniques of other (usually successful) writers. They ask questions like: Should you write in the morning or evening (as though your book really cares)? Can you use longhand, transcription or a computer? How many rewrites must you do? In most cases, the more you read about writing, the less likely you'll actually complete something. Oh, yes, you'll start – maybe – but you won't finish. By searching for the right method, it helps you by delaying the actual writing process, which is the goal of most writers anyhow. That's right, most writers will tell you they hate sitting down to write. OK, hate is a strong term. However, they would rather play chess over the Internet, read an interesting newspaper article, scan their portfolio, or daydream about the lost love that got away. See where I'm going? The biggest difference between the pros and the wannabees is that the pros sit down and do it one word at a time. Amateurs write, and wannabees think about wanting to write. I'll save you tons of time. It really doesn't matter whether you write when you wake up, on the bus, in pencil, on a notebook or by dictating your material. I read that Nobel Laureate Ernest Hemingway wrote standing up, while Nobel Laureate Eugene O'Neill NEVER wrote again when arthritis prevented him from handwriting on paper with No. 2 pencils – he dismissed dictation and typing. A friend of mine told me that Col. David H. Hackworth was so time-pressed for writing that he taped a notebook to his thigh and wrote one paragraph each day as he drove to his Pentagon office. From there his secretary would type up his paragraph, they'd go over it throughout the day, and he'd start all over the next day. Talk about writing a book one paragraph at a time. In fiction, I've read that best-selling author Scott Turow would write his book on the train going into and out of Chicago. You try writing on a train. I can understand jotting down a few paragraphs going into work, but going home at the end of the day when you're tired? Every day? Whew! That's commitment.

The Case For Self-Publishing. Now to make a case for self-publishing with a slight preamble. Twenty years ago I wouldn't have made this recommendation, and I'm not totally sure that I would have made it 10 years ago. Times change. While proponents of self-publishing often point out famous authors who self-published (like Tom Paine and Ben Franklin), the reality was that if you self-published, you weren't a real author. That's no longer true, especially in nonfiction. The entire communications process, because of the Internet and the electronic age, has changed how we view, process and deliver information. In the past, I'd bet money that you could give me 10 books and I'd be able to tell which one was self-published. Invariably, the quality of paper and cover had a cheap look, and the design had an amateurish quality to it that was obvious. Today, you often can't tell the difference. If the author uses a different name for his "publishing" company so that it's not identified with him, you have even less association with self-publishing. In other words, in the "old" days, Bob Matterhorn would write a book, and the publisher would be

Matterhorn Publishing. It didn't take a genius to figure out that Bob Matterhorn published his own book.

But back to basics. Why self-publish (as I have)? Let's start by comparing it with the reasons you might want to go with a publishing house, as I mentioned earlier.

Control. You write what you want, as you want to write it, with the font size that pleases you. You also get to pick the title (actually, publishers are probably better at this than most writers). The point is that if a publisher dislikes the way you said things (leaving aside obvious issues of libel that no one could defend), you're probably going to have to convince the publisher that you're right. In the end, he's usually right (even though you're the writer), because he holds the money strings. When you self-publish, you have an approval audience of one: yourself. I've taken a decided tone or attitude in this book, in case you haven't noticed by now. I've done this for several reasons, but mostly because I wanted to write a book that was as honest as I could make it. After a career of writing where I tried to be as objective and in the background as much as possible, I simply got tired of it. I really am, in many ways, the way I sound in this book. My honest-to-goodness goal is to teach you something about publicity. Period. If I've entertained you along the way, great. If not, if I've irritated or offended you by my style or approach, tough shit, that's your problem, not mine. I've read many books that had valuable information, but the writing was so boring you just couldn't wade through it all. Good writers know an unassailable truth: When you try to please everyone, you've usually reduced the writing to pabulum. I confess that if I submitted this book to a mainstream publisher, it's doubtful, despite the wealth of information, that many would permit my irreverent style. I would have to justify it. When I self-publish, however, I'm in control.

Timing. I published this book a few days after I made the final proofing changes. That means, because of the physical makeup of the book, I was able to have copies available in a few days. With a publisher, how long would you be waiting? Well, as I mentioned earlier, it could be between three months and up to one year. In some cases it's even longer. You could be dead before you ever see your book on a bookshelf.

Freshness. My goal is to update this book every year or two. Obviously, that means cutting out old, dated material and adding information, but it probably doesn't include a complete rewrite. The point is that I can make changes when I feel I'm ready. It's unlikely that a mainstream publisher would allow for minor changes each year unless you had a whopping bestseller on your hands or you had planned to update it annually. It's a cost issue, and for mainstream publishers it makes sense. It's easier and cheaper just to keep issuing the book they have already. For me, the costs are only minimal, depending on any slight increases in printing that I have to absorb. In a sense, all self-published authors are in the custom publishing business, which means they publish a product – in this case, a book – on demand.

Money. In many cases, if you want to enjoy the positive economics of a book, you should self-publish, if you believe you can eventually market your own book. **This is a critical distinction but probably the most important one from a monetary standpoint.** You keep only 10 percent of the book's retail price if you go with a traditional publisher (and don't forget that your agent, if you have one, will get 10 to 15 percent of your fee). With a self-published book, you keep all the profit after expenses. How much is that? Let me give you a real-life example. I know an expert who wrote and self-published a book for a specific industry and audience. His "book" is about 50 pages, and he provides a cassette tape, where he reads the contents of the book. (He claims people in his industry don't read.) He sells the book for $49. It costs him about $5 to create the book, including the professionally produced cassette. For the sake of example, a book that sells for $20 might cost between 10 and 20 percent of the retail price to produce, plus whatever money you spend on marketing. I realize that your goal is to promote yourself and your book, but it doesn't hurt to make a few bucks while you're trying to obtain publicity. This is the other aspect of why writing a book makes sense if you have the personality for it. While all my methods of gaining publicity are almost free, it does cost you at least a few dollars to publish your own book. A book can earn money for you, no matter who publishes it.

If you're going to self-publish, you can pay to have it done professionally as a package. This is risky, and I DO NOT recommend this for beginners. Let's say you order 2,000 books at $7 each. You've shelled out $14,000. You push the books, but for whatever reason never sell more than 25 percent of the 2,000 you ordered. You gross $10,000, which still leaves you $4,000 in the hole. If you're satisfied with being a published expert, which has great cachet value, and you have an almost limitless supply of books to use for promotion purposes, then you're fine. If you don't want to or can't afford to "lose" this money, it's risky.

The other approach is to create each book as you need it, or at least no more than 50 to 100 at a time. Let's say you've written a 150-page book. Cost at Kinko's (as of this writing) is 8 cents per page. Tack on $1 for a heavier paper cover and spiral binding, and you're paying $13 for the book, which you sell for $20. The difference is that you can literally "create" these books to order and start with an initial order of one or 100. My recommendation: If you're starting out and don't know anything about the publishing business but are capable of putting a book-length manuscript together, publish it at the lowest-possible price until you gain confidence and understand the business. This way you won't lose money. Believe me, when you see it only costs about $3 to publish a book (for a minimum 3,000 order), you might get tempted to plop down the requisite cost. Authors who have one or two thousand of their books in closets, basements, attics and storage abound. Worse, some of the information in these books becomes dated, and you can't give them away. Keeping the 3,000 initial run for your book scenario in mind, let me explain what happens. "Natural forces" occur, which means you have a publicity campaign and all your relatives, friends, neighbors, ex-lovers and grade school classmates buy your book. A few hundred sell because of the publicity campaign. What happens to the rest? You get to keep those books as part of your own private library.

Last thought about self-publishing. Self-publishing, especially if you really start to sell your book, gives you enormous strength if you go to a mainline publisher to make a deal. Now you've answered the second question that every publisher has. That is: Can this person deliver a manuscript? (The first question is whether the book will sell.) When you plop your book on the table and brag about selling 10,000 copies during the past two years, you'll get their attention. (How do you prove you sold 10,000 copies? You open your financial records to the publishing house.) I want a major publisher to recognize that I can finish a book, market it and understand the economics of publishing. If I don't get a good deal, I'm simply not interested. Again, the key is whether you're prepared to market your book (and expertise) at the same time. I love it. Some people hate it. It's up to you. Just make sure your lawyer looks at the contract if you get a major publisher and be sure to send me an autographed copy (for free) because I told you so.

If you are going to self-publish and don't read Dan Poynter's book, *The Self-Publishing Manual: How to Write, Print and Sell Your Own Book,* you should have your brain examined for air leakage. Get the latest edition. (I have the 14th edition.) It's the best book on the subject. No discussion. (Available at www.parapublishing.com or toll free 805-PARAPUB (727-2782).) Tell Dan that I sent you.

The same recommendation holds for marketing your book. John Kremer's 700+ pages *1001 Ways to Market Your*

Books is an indispensable guide for reaching your intended audience (and those you didn't intend). It's a complete marketing program in one volume. (Available at www.bookmarket.com or 800-796-6130). Tell John I sent you.

Tom's Unassailable, Absolute, Infallible Rule For Writing. If there's any first commandment to the writing business, this is it: Virtually every writer of note whose techniques I'm familiar with establishes a (somewhat) rigid pattern for writing and sticks to it. It's as easy and as difficult as that. Some people (like me) set a time minimum. About one-third of the way through the first draft for this book, I began using a stopwatch. One hour (minimum). I could write longer or twice in a day if the inclination hit me. Nonetheless, no matter what, I had to spend at least one hour a day, five days a week on the book, even if I finished only one sentence in that hour. (Yes, if the phone rang and I decided to answer it, I stopped the stopwatch.)

Some writers establish word minimums (1,000 words a day) or a page minimum (four pages a day, which actually works out to about 1,000 words). I know one author who has written seven business books. Her approach is to set aside two weeks each year. Once a year, she checks into a hotel for two weeks and writes her book. Of course, she's collecting, shifting and thinking about the material throughout the year. Presumably, she's also outlined the book before she actually begins to write. She's unusual in this case. I've never met a writer who completed a book by writing it when inspiration hit. Virtually all writers complete books by adhering to a schedule. I'm sure there might be one percent of writers (though I doubt it's that high) who wait for inspiration. If you trust me on anything, trust me on this: Dear reader, you're NOT in the one percent.

Does all this book-writing technique really work? Midway through this chapter, I stopped to have bagels with my son, Andrew (who's off from school). We went back home, picked up my notebook computer, drove to the bank, made a deposit, then walked to the library where Andrew toyed with the library's computer while I returned to working on my book. The Italians have a phrase that explains it this way: La Dolce Vita. The Good Life.

Chapter 9

Writing Articles For Promoting Yourself

Short, Sweet & Successful

I spent most of the last chapter talking about writing a book because it really does put you in a class of your own. Nevertheless it doesn't have to be a choice between a book or nothing at all. Many experts contribute articles to various magazines and write about their areas of expertise. That's how they become experts. Then something strange and really wonderful happens. If you write enough articles, especially in the same publication, sooner or later the phone rings or you get an e-mail asking for your help on a project or for you to appear as a speaker. Anyone can write an article if you can put simple sentences together. (You can write a book too, as I pointed out.) I'm not going to give you a course on article writing. Books and libraries abound with good advice. (See Appendix.) The only advice that I will add is have someone look at your copy BEFORE you turn it into the editor. Yes, it's his job, but be smart and make his job easier.

Since I believe that virtually anyone can be a published author, the logical question is: What publications should I consider? The best listings for a potential market for your articles or press releases is your own media list, mentioned in Chapter 5. Remember, you decided that this media list most accurately reflects the audience that you want to influence. If you have a very large list and divided the list into A (most important), B (important), and C (less important) groups, you'll simply want to contact each publication to see whether they accept freelance or bylined articles. In all likelihood, they do. That means they'll consider an article or a submission from a writer who is not on staff.

The best general listing for potential markets – including publications of which you've never heard – is *Writer's Market 2004* (updated annually). (The media resources I mentioned in Chapter 5 also have large lists of publications.) The cost is only about $30, and every bookstore (and library) has a copy. Most freelance writers consider this to be the information bible for finding publications that pay for articles. Published by Writer's Digest Books, this reference gives you the lowdown on thousands of potential markets. However, it only includes publications that pay. This is important because if you're interested in writing for trade publications in order to increase your visibility, these types of magazines often don't pay for articles. (Writer's Digest also has a large listing of trade publications, too, but only those that pay for freelance articles.)

How Do You Know What Editors Want? You know the audience that you wish to influence and you're reasonably sure that the magazine you have in front of you addresses that group. How can you be sure this publication targets the readers that you want to influence? If you don't know, obtain a copy of the publication's media kit. In there, it usually lists the demographic background for the sake of potential advertisers. It's an invaluable source for discovering who reads the publication. Let's say that you're in the home improvement business and you're the owner of Harriett's Home Improvement Solutions. What next?

Step 1: First, you get an A for the name. Someone probably knows what you do because of the name you've chosen. A second line would help, such as, "solving home improvement problems at a reasonable cost". You've just answered another question about your business: Are you affordable? When using public relations, it's still amazing how people want to promote the name of their business or organization, but when it stands alone, no one has a clue about what it does. That means if you haven't decided on a name or if there is still time to change your name, this is the time to do it. Yes, I break this very rule with my own company name, Galileo Communications Inc. But I don't go after the consumer market, and my referral business is, fortunately, so strong that I've never found the need to explain explicitly what I do. People never call me out of the blue to inquire about my publicity or editorial skills. They come to me as a referral or because they read an article I wrote or bought this book. (Yes, I follow my own advice when it comes to writing.) A company name that is easy to remember and one that explains what you do is helpful in your publicity efforts.

Step 2: Look at *Writer's Market* to see if they list magazines in the category that interests you and examine each magazine's editorial needs. Or go to each magazine's Web site to see whether they post their editorial guidelines. Not all magazines post editorial guidelines, but if they do, you must look at them. Editorial guidelines are simply rules established by the magazine for would-be writers. Examining a publication's guidelines is so important that it's suicide to try to become a well-published expert if you don't follow this procedure. Finding editorial guidelines is akin to being in writer's heaven because the editor, in essence, is telling you exactly how to pitch (sell) your story idea.

Step 3: Always look at the editorial calendar of any publication you are considering sending an article or story idea. I virtually NEVER pitch an idea to a magazine without first reviewing its editorial calendar. Let me explain. In the fall of each year, the magazine staff sits down and decides the type of stories that will run the following year. They might not have a specific idea, but they'll be thinking of general themes and topics. The editorial calendar will also list the month or issue in which this story, theme or topic will appear. This also applies to regular columns, features or "beats" that run in the magazine. Seldom will an editorial calendar list every article for the upcoming year because at monthly (usually) editorial meetings, editors decide on editorial content or articles. Ideas that crop up during the year in editorial meetings usually focus on timing issues or simply pop up as a good idea during brainstorming sessions. Very little activity can be more creative than a good or great editorial meeting. Ideas explode like firecrackers, and it's fun to push the idea envelope until the top person – the editor-in-chief or the publisher – looks at you as though you're crazy. This is how stories appear in magazines: partly through pre-planned editorial calendars and partly through spontaneous ideas that writers and editors agree upon during editorial meetings. The percentage of this breakdown is so exclusive to the magazine that I won't even venture a guess unless I have the magazine in front of me. Taken to its extremes, you could write an editorial calendar for the magazine that would encompass the entire upcoming year and never deviate from it. Or you could publish a magazine without an editorial calendar. I'll venture a guess, and this is strictly anecdotal, that editorial calendars list between 20 and 50 percent of the articles that will appear the following year. I'm harping on editorial calendars for a basic reason. They are an indispensable way of knowing what the magazine will write about and in which issue it will appear. It also allows you to pitch a story for March in December (which is not too soon). Never ignore deadlines. Magazines operate about two to four months (sometimes more) ahead of the issue that you buy on the newsstand. These days, virtually every magazine has an editorial calendar that you can view and download from the Internet. Magazine sales staff also uses the calendar to sell advertisement "around" the topic. For example, if a magazine intends to publish a section on new computers, you can bet that the salespeople will contact the major computer manufacturers with the goal of including them as advertisers.

If the magazine doesn't have an online editorial calendar, try *Writer's Market*. Always look for the writer's guidelines.

Step 4: Buy a copy of the magazine or go to the library and take a peek. Today you can also probably access the magazine on the Web (unless it's very small) and examine it. Nothing beats a copy of the magazine, because, while many publications are now on the Internet, they seldom post the current issue in full. Because you're not privy to editorial meetings, you don't know what's being included into the publication. With the magazine in hand, you'll be able to examine every possible category in the magazine that might have an interest or impact in your quest for publicity. This is an easy way to familiarize yourself with the publication. You want to know the nature of the articles, the tone, topics, length, whether they use artwork (photos, drawings, clip art, etc.), what the tagline looks like, etc.

If you're in the business-to-business field, you're really lucky. That means that trade publications, magazines directed to specific industries, probably cover your area. The good news is that many of them are free. Just go to their Web site or get a copy and fill in a card that offers a free subscription. I don't need any more weights in my office. I work out with the cartons that contain the trade publications I receive.

Examine the masthead. This is the section of the publication that lists the people who work for it. Don't direct your idea to the publisher (unless it is a smaller magazine and shares the editor's title). I usually aim my queries in this order: 1) If it's a small magazine, I go directly for the editor; 2) If the magazine has a managing editor (ME), they're the ones to whom I send my queries or press releases. That's because the ME serves as the traffic cop on most magazines. They often have the most complete, current overview of what is occurring, from story ideas under consideration to the writing assignments for various staff and freelance writers. (The editors at large magazines often play a public relations role as well as an editorial role. The ME is usually in the trenches getting the work done.); 3) Special editors. This applies to a columnist, for example, who covers a beat, topic or industry. I advise some small businesses about publicity. If a magazine has a small-business editor, that person would be the one who should receive my press releases. Use common sense. If the magazine has a product release editor and you have a product release, guess who gets it. The product release editor. In doubt about to whom you should direct your pitch for writing an article (or sending a press release)? Call up the magazine or send an e-mail and ask. They don't bite. It's a practice I follow frequently.

Tom's Tip: The best time to approach an editor is when they're new on the job. They haven't developed a thick skin yet, probably don't have a fixed notion of how to do things and, in a very real sense, need some "help" in establishing themselves. Watch for any changes in the masthead, especially the editor's column where he writes about how happy he is to be aboard and the direction in which he wants to guide the magazine. The key is that no editor is ever as open-minded about accepting story ideas or articles for a publication as when he first comes aboard. Also, if you follow a publication because it has special interest for you – a magazine that you wish to appear in – keep in mind that these opportunities occur more often than you'd think. Today, people in general change jobs frequently, and in journalism, I'd venture to say that it happens even more frequently because of the nature of the job and the generally low pay. Always stay on good terms with editors regardless of the level at which they serve.

Talented editors go to other magazines, which might become another publication target for you, and lower-ranked editors often get promoted to the top of the masthead (associate editors become managing editors and managing editors become the editor). I can't tell you how often this approach has worked for me.

Step 5: Be sure the publication publishes the type of article that you're proposing to write. This goes back to obtaining a copy of the magazine, examining it online and getting a copy of its editorial calendar. **The most frequent mistake that beginners make when submitting ideas or articles is that they simply don't bother to understand the magazine's audience and how editors interpret the needs of that group.** For example, if a magazine focuses on the restaurant business and never publishes recipes, it's foolish to send an article about how to make a perfect soufflé in five minutes. It just won't work. It's amazing how often someone shoots off an idea or article and thinks that maybe "this" editor will use it. Bridge clubs are not a platform for public speaking, and a Toastmaster's club is not the place for a bridge tournament. There is one exception to this rule, and I generally hesitate to mention it. A few very savvy publicity people will write an article which they believe will serve a large audience. They will then submit the article to <u>many</u> trade publications. This occasionally works in the trade press and almost never in the consumer press. (For the record, consumer publications are those you see at the magazine stand: women's, men's, beauty, sports and some general business publications. Trade publications cover a specific industry.) Here's an example. I know a fellow who specializes in sales and distribution across many industries, ranging from durable to consumable goods. He'll write an article that's about sales (now that's a broad topic) and send it to several hundred magazines that he thinks might be interested in using it. This is time-consuming and costs money if you do it with a mailing. It takes time, but with e-mail it doesn't cost as much and shrinks the physical task of delivering/sending the articles. Fortunately, he has an assistant to take care of this chore. Also, remember that many editors will consider an unsolicited article as Spam. For most people, this approach won't work. The sales and distribution expert with whom I'm familiar told me he has about a 5 percent rate of acceptance.

Step 6: Once you've decided on the type of article you want to write, you have two choices: Write the entire article by yourself (or your ghostwriter) or send a query letter proposing the idea to an editor. A query letter is simply a one- or two-page letter to an editor suggesting a story that you would like to write for their publication. I'd suggest that you use queries, especially if there is a narrow interest for the piece you're proposing. The problem with writing a completed article is that it's a zero-sum game. If someone doesn't publish it, you've lost time writing it with no place for it to appear. This can be particularly discouraging if you find writing to be a laborious process. It's much easier to write a query letter and mail or e-mail it to an editor and begin writing the article after an editor gives you the green light.

Step 7: How do you write a query letter? There are literally dozens (if not hundreds) of books about how to pique an editor's interest – in short, writing a query letter. It's effortless to describe but not easy to do. First, keep it to one page whenever possible. Never go beyond two pages. Second, write a headline, just as you would for the article. (We call that a "working head" because it'll probably change later.) If you can't write a headline, then you don't know what your topic is or it's too broad. You must narrow it down to a headline. Third, write that all-important first paragraph to grab the editor's attention. Give the reasons why the idea is good, what's new and fresh about it, and reassure the editor that you'll deliver. You might not have the experience to use this line, but I always finish with something to this effect: "Because I've been a journalist for more than 20 years, I'll turn in copy that's tight and bright [an old-fashioned, favorite newspaper expression] and on deadline. I'll also provide all the artwork you need [I only use this line when I'm capable of sending photos, diagrams and so on that should accompany the manuscript]. And I never miss a deadline." ***PLEASE*** don't copy my approach or I'll hunt you down for retribution. Use one that fits you. **If you're writing a query in response to the editorial calendar, be sure to mention that your topic is directed toward the subject which the editorial calendar lists for the April issue, for example.** Timing is important, too, when using the editorial calendar. On average, editors work two to four months ahead (or "out" as they like to say).

Step 8: Write the article and submit it. OK, you got the assignment, now what? You **must** meet the deadline which you and your editor agreed upon for the article, and you should write to the standard of the articles published in the magazine. If you fail to meet the deadline or if your prose is so turgid that the editor either rejects it outright or has to slave over it to repair the damage, you probably won't get another shot at appearing in the publication. (It's infrequent that an editor "kills" a story. If the editor didn't feel you could deliver, he wouldn't have assigned it.) It's often a good idea about halfway through an assignment to send a note or e-mail to the editor reminding him that you're on schedule and will meet the deadline you've promised. This is especially important if you've never worked for the editor before. They're human. They need to be reassured.

Tom's Tip: Write a tagline for yourself and be sure to include a way for people to contact you. This might be the most important part of the article. After all, you're creating this article so that your name gets out there, but if people can't reach you, why bother? As a rule, most editors in the past did not include a way for readers to reach a writer, except in some trade publications. Things are changing. In the trade press, those magazines designed for the business-to-business audience in a specific field, industry or profession have often been favorable about including a tagline, and sometimes they're even generous about allowing the writer (you) to describe the services or products that you or your company offer. The consumer press has always been much more resistant to this. The trend seems to be to allow writers to have their tagline include an e-mail address. **Always, *always*, on anything that's printed, allow the reader to reach you without effort or cost.** I simply cannot stress this enough. In the past, readers virtually never wrote to writers. It just took too much effort, and a response might come weeks later. With e-mail, it's instant feedback and often instant response. For example, if you sell forest-firefighting equipment and wrote an article about the latest technology in forest firefighting, you might end the article with a tagline like this: Joe Smith, a former forest firefighter, is president of Cheyenne, Wyoming-based Extinguish The Fires. He can be reached at joesmith@extinquishthefires.com or at (999) 999-9999.

Tom's Tip: Never write anything for public consumption without an identifying tagline that allows readers to contact you. **Never!**

Chapter 10

The Information Tip Sheet

Here's My Best Tip About Free Publicity

Drum Roll. Attention, please. I'm about to give you the single best way to influence journalists and, in the process, garner publicity for yourself. **Tip sheets are the most-effective, least-used technique for obtaining publicity**. A tip sheet is nothing more than a list (seldom more than three) of story ideas for journalists. It's a wonder that more individuals or groups don't use them with greater frequency (though I am seeing a few more recently). Maybe it's because they're so easy that no one believes something this obvious can be so effective, because nothing delivers your ideas to the media, during an extended period of time, with more punch than the tip sheet.

There are actually two types of tip sheets: information tip sheets and idea tip sheets. The more common of the two is the information tip sheet. This is simply a document of one to three pages that offers basic information about an idea, product or service that you want to promote. As always, it's best to keep an information tip sheet to a few pages. In brief, think of it as a short article, a quick read with plenty of pizzazz, tidbits of information and a flourish for an ending. Information tip sheets offer practical and useful information, insight and opinion on a topic in a pithy format that is easily digestible for the reader. In this case, the reader is the journalist who receives it. The best information tip sheets lead the reporter or editor to seek, no, hunger for, more information. When you've created that hunger, the only recourse is for the journalist to call you for more information until he has satisfied the need for more facts. The best part of an information tip sheet, when written correctly, is that it can be used "as is," thus actually becoming a story or filler. And it's not even a press release. There are three ways to write the information tip sheet. We'll take each in turn.

Information Tip Sheet Style One: The Tease. You offer only a paragraph or two of information, in essence saying that a tip sheet exists, it's about this topic, and if you want more information, call, write, e-mail, etc. This is probably the least-effective approach because an editor is less likely to use it as a filler, and there isn't enough for a story based on the actual tip(s). Still, this approach is better than doing nothing or a humdrum press release. Let's say you own a karate school and want to mention that you're offering free guidelines about how to defend yourself. You offer these guidelines in a pamphlet and use the tip sheet to make the offer through the media. The goal is to have the media run the offer, driving readers to write, call or visit your Web site for the self-defense pamphlet. The problem with using a "tease" approach in the information tip sheet is that even if you *have* an interesting topic, you're still forcing the journalist who is interested in your topic to make an extra effort to get the information. They either have to make a call, write a note or log onto the Internet. An editor might use your offer as a filler or pop it into a section devoted to trivia or updates. Indeed, *The Contest Newsletter* in the late 1970s grew to one of the largest newsletters in the United States by simply offering a sample copy of its newsletter as long as a self-addressed, stamped envelope (SASE) accompanied the request. The problem with the tease approach is that the editor won't know the quality of the information and whether it's solid material or a thinly disguised sales pitch. Editors hate it when someone uses them for blatant commercialism. If you're going to use the "tease" approach, enclosing a copy of your pamphlet or tip sheet that you're offering the public will help overcome an editor's skepticism.

Information Tip Sheet Style Two: Half The Glory. In this approach, you mention the same "tease" for free information. You actually offer a number of the tips that readers can expect to find in your pamphlet or on your Web site without providing all the information. Going back to our karate school example, in addition to saying the information tip sheet exists, you also say that it offers the 10 most-effective ways to throw a punch so that you can protect yourself. You explain that Joe's Karate Emporium is offering a tip sheet on the 10 cardinal rules for throwing a karate punch. This is something, of course, that every grade-schooler will want to learn so they can practice on their cohorts as they line up for third-grade class. It will make the mothers happy to know that those punches will now have quality AND effectiveness.

You write it like this:

10 Secrets To Throwing The Perfect Karate Punch

Tip 1: Roll your fingers into a ball until you have a tight fist.

Tip 2: Keep your wrist straight. Do not bend it.

Tip 3: Check to see that you have a 90 degree right angle between the back of your hand and the back of your fingers, which are now in a clenched-fist formation.

Tip 4: Make sure that you keep your fist near your torso.

For the remainder of the 10 Secrets To Throwing The Perfect Karate Punch, contact Joe Kikster at 1-800-888-KICK or send an e-mail to Joe@kicksandinyourface.com.

What you've done here is quite simple. You've shared some valuable information with your reader and you're teasing the reader in the hopes that he will take the next step and contact you. You're also teasing the editor because you're hoping that he'll publish this part-informational, part-tease tip sheet in his magazine.

I saw this partial information tip sheet concept used recently on the Internet in a press release format. The style of presentation of the release was ho-hum, but they had the right idea. They started off offering tips from a world-renowned expert. This type of approach and the effectiveness of using superlatives has lessened because we're so inured against hyperbole – especially with a sophisticated audience. Get to the benefit or hook immediately or you'll lose the reader.

You also run a risk with this type of tip information sheet. You've softened up the reader and now you're literally "forcing" him to take an action that creates more work. Would you serve someone half a sandwich and tell them they have to get up and go to another table if they want the remainder? Unless the person really wants the information, my feeling about this approach is that you will evoke some positive feelings but also heighten negative ones. It's similar to what people say about Notre Dame. You either love 'em or hate 'em but you're seldom neutral.

Information Tip Sheet Style Three: The Whole Enchilada. This tip sheet follows the same formula as No. 2 except that you include all the information. In short, you write a mini-article disguised as a tip sheet. This approach is my favorite because it allows you to present the strongest "argument" when pitching the tip sheet to a journalist, with you as the "expert" in the story. You can end this tip sheet by stating or implying that more information is available from you, the expert. This allows them to contact you for an expanded article or to simply use the information you've provided as a stand-alone, mini-article.

An editor has four choices of what to do with your tip sheet. First, he can trash your tip sheet for an infinite number of reasons – it just doesn't fit, he doesn't care about the topic, he's too busy to bother, etc. Second, he can take the tip sheet and store it in his idea file (we'll discuss this vital file later). Third, he can run your tip sheet or mini-article as is, including the tagline or ending which directs people to you. Ultimately this is always your goal: influencing your target market. Fourth, he can cut or reduce your tip sheet and publish a shortened version, or he can even call you to ask for more information for an expanded article.

Tom's Tip: Whenever possible, I would go with the **Information Tip Sheet Style No. Three: The Whole Enchilada**. That is, give all the information that you're willing to share. I firmly believe that this approach raises the possibility that an editor will use the information in your tip sheet for their publication and create enough of an interest for the editor to give you a call.

If you want a publicity campaign that is down and dirty, that means the least effort, the least fuss, write a one-page **Information Tip Sheet Style No. One: The Tease**. Just be sure that if you're asking people to respond for more information, you have it available – immediately – whether that means a pamphlet, photocopied "report" or posting to a Web site. I've seen tons of marketing efforts that offer a free "report." That report is often nothing more than a one-page sheet. Is it a rip-off? Not if it fills a need and is free. I think this is a great idea. Radio guru Alex Carroll offers a free, one-page report on speed traps in your state. If you live in New Jersey and this one-page report carries a listing of those speed traps, who cares what it looks like as long as the information is useful, clear and easy to follow?

The Idea Tip Sheet. Welcome to graduate school, because this is where we separate the men and women from the boys and girls. There's another way to publicize your expertise without actually having a tip sheet of information ideas (those of you who hate the idea of writing will love this one). Create a tip sheet of story ideas related to the subject for which you're seeking publicity and nothing more. You're enticing the journalist to call and interview you if he's interested in pursuing the story. In other words, you're not going through the process of writing a short article laden with tips and then sending that quasi-article, or part of that article, to an editor. Here, all you do is sit back and wait for the editor to contact you.

Here's how to write idea tip sheets.

Step 1: Never submit more than three ideas to an editor. It's the old but effective sales cliché about giving people choices. I tend to favor three ideas at a time, but two is OK. A good editor quickly knows whether ideas are interesting and solid or whether they're fluff. Don't forget: You must answer the "Why Should I Care?" question explained in Chapter 7.

Step 2: Write the headline of the story idea you're proposing. For example, back to our karate school story, when I try to write a headline, I realize that I'm not sure you could weave a story around making a fist. Here is a quick story idea.

Martial Arts Improves Kids' Grade Average. Kids who study martial arts increase their grade point average by an average of one grade in half of the courses they take, according to Bob Welch, a martial arts expert and director of Welch's Martial Arts Academy in Cherry Hill.

"Martial Arts isn't just about punching and kicking, it's about improving performance in other aspects of kids' lives," says Welch, who carefully tracks the academic performance of his students.

Welch would be happy to explain the connection between improved grades and martial arts training. Call Bob at (555) 555-5555 for more information to arrange an interview or send him an e-mail at bobwelchkarate.com.

Notice a few things. I kept the idea to THREE paragraphs. You'd better have a good reason to write longer. Take note that with this length, I can get TWO story ideas to a page. Because of the length, it took me fewer than five minutes to write this idea. How's that for being efficient? Finally, this idea will appeal to EVERY editor who has an audience where the focus is on family, parents or children. It could also appeal to a sports editor or an Op-Ed page editor. Obviously, it's not the kind of idea I would send to a business magazine. Could it appeal to a local parenting magazine? It's simply perfect.

Tom's Tip: It's all about the idea folder. Why all this fuss about the tip sheet? Easy answer. Every journalist worth his salt has an idea file. Sure, some journalists might give it a different label, they might be irregular about saving ideas, this folder might exist (these days) in electronic or digital format, but everyone has days where the ideas just don't come. Pretend you're the journalist. You scream, you look to the heavens for inspiration, you stare blankly outside your window for untold minutes, but no matter what you do, you can't seem to generate a solid, fresh story idea. This becomes even uglier during a budget or editorial meeting when journalists gather with their peers to discuss that day's newspaper stories or next month's magazine ideas. No one wants to attend these meetings and look like a dullard. Remember what we said earlier: There's news and then there's stuff. Again, the "real" news will be obvious, but the stuff, if saved in an idea file, might become news. I continue to serve as an editor of two national magazines directed to a specific industry and keep an idea folder for each. I also keep an idea folder for every client. (I've given instructions in my will to put a blank idea folder in my coffin, just in case.) I always kept an idea folder when I worked as an editor for a daily newspaper and as a writer and editor on a variety of magazines.

Most journalists, except for the very new or those completed burned out, recognize the need, practicality and salvation of keeping an idea folder. That's where you hope the tip sheet disappears: right into the idea folder if the journalist doesn't use it immediately. Don't allow your tip sheet to share the same fate of most time-sensitive press releases: a trip to the trash basket or extinguished by the tap of the delete key. That's why tip sheets should generally have an "evergreen" (a common magazine term) feel about them. A journalist can use them any time. They stay (theoretically) fresh forever.

Tom's Tip: A Checklist For Tip Sheets

Regardless of the type of tip sheet you send out – information or idea – don't break these rules:

- **When sending an information tip sheet** with a partial idea or your mini-story, **DON'T** send a second idea. Keep it to a single thought. DON'T send any other tips. Be sure to keep your page count down to no more than three pages. I STRONGLY recommend keeping it to one or two pages.
- **Write a real grabber of a headline.** If you question the effectiveness of your headline, ask someone who has media experience. Make sure the headline grabs the editor's attention. Then lead the journalist to the body of the tip sheet where he can satisfy his thirst for more information. Write the tip sheet just like a story. My close friend and outstanding criminal defense attorney, Michael Karnavas, [If you're ever charged with a serious crime, this is the guy you want handling the defense. As I write this, he's at The Hague defending a client against crimes against humanity] who once shared the platform with another well-known criminal defense attorney, recalls the advice his famous counterpart gave when giving a closing argument. He advised: "Make it sound like a cheap dime novel."

The point? Make sure the journalist can't put it down.

- **Be SURE to place all pertinent information for contacting you at the end of the tip sheet.** For example, if you're offering information for free to the public and you want them to pay for the envelope and postage (if you're offering printed material), make sure that you mention they should include a self-addressed, stamped envelope (SASE). Obviously, you'll want to include your phone number, fax number (if relevant), e-mail address and Web site.

Tom's Tip: *Sending out tip sheets on a regular basis is the most important publicity-seeking activity you can implement.* Decide in advance how often you're going to send tip sheets to the media and hold to that schedule no matter what. It might take a year or more to embed your tip sheets into the minds of the journalists you want to influence. Be relentless – sooner or later, they'll use your tip sheet if you offer good information. What I usually recommend is a monthly tip sheet or a quarterly issue tied to a season so that if you're late a week or two, no one notices. It also extends the "shelf" life of the tip sheet if someone picks it up. For example, you could have a spring, summer, fall, winter tip sheet. It's a nice fit. After a while, if your tips are good – even if the journalist doesn't use them – I can assure you that he'll open the envelope when he sees it and will read it.

I get dozens of newsletters, which are the overburdened cousin of the tip sheet. Guess which ones I read and which ones I dump? No surprise, but I read the ones that deliver good, solid information. It's surprising how many people forget this obvious lesson. And the reason they forget is because they really think that improving its appearance or jazzing it up with graphics will overcome the handicap of little or no content. Invariably they're wrong.

Do tip sheets work? If you do nothing else for publicity and are involved in a service or product that can generate a few ideas each year, then send out tip sheets.

A True Story: Tell us, Tom, does this stuff really work? An editor of a major trade publication recently joined the magazine. I managed to have her accept a story idea, which we would write (remember how more approachable a new editor is). Separately, my client sent this editor a tip sheet with three ideas. Just a list of potential ideas that they might consider using. (Yes, reader, this is a great client who listens and follows his publicity expert's advice.) The editor promptly chose two of the tip sheet ideas for stories and assigned them to my client. Now that's a total of THREE stories, two from tip sheets. This is a very important publication directed to the audience that my client wishes to influence.

Tip sheets work. For the few who know their power, nothing works better.

Chapter 11

Newsy Newsletters

Transforming A Standard Into Something Special

Is there any public relations person who *doesn't* recommend a newsletter? And don't they proliferate? Then asks the wise woman: Why are so many so *bad*?

Sending out your newsletter to current and potential clients and customers is a must if you can afford the cost. Sending out a newsletter to the media or other persons who you want to influence is also a must, provided that you've thought through the way they perceive your newsletter.

First, though, let's start with the purpose of the newsletter. It's to provide information (news, that's why they call it a newsletter) in a succinct, easy-to-read, digestible format that is low on fluff and appearance and high on content. Newsletters that are effective must be informative, interesting and engaging in a brisk way. Most newsletters that people ask me to examine or redo are either boring, lack personality or are downright dreadful. I'll concede that the "look" of newsletters has improved from 10 or 20 years ago. Given today's "smarter" software, even homegrown newsletters can demonstrate a reasonable appearance. (Though too many people take a stab at it and turn out dreadful examples.) But it's the content that's the killer. Let's be blunt. No one is going to read a newsletter for its appearance. Especially in an age when newsletters with a modest audience can look extremely "professional" because of inexpensive software, the ability to separate your newsletter from others has decreased. Most now have a certain indefinable look that we unconsciously recognize. Nor are readers (and the media) looking for information of novella length. Readers want sharp, sassy, pertinent, helpful, insightful, reference-type material they can use, store or toss quickly.

The biggest sin that most newsletters commit is that it's all about you. I should make a distinction here. Company newsletters for employees might be OK when it comes to the self-aggrandizement that most newsletters employ. Fine. It's the company, you're the employee, so in theory, at least, you're the company or a part of the company (except maybe when it's time to dish out stock options). Newsletters that you direct to current and potential customers and clients (and the media) must offer information. They simply don't care about your receiving an award from the Church Of What Isn't Happening Now for your contribution of 25 legal pads. If you're a jeweler, they might be far more interested in the (predicted) hottest new stones for the next decade.

I've noticed that more newsletters make some effort in this direction but still can't get across the finish line. Now they don't totally spend their time bragging and actually offer – maybe – an article or two of interest. Invariably, they weaken their hand and their credibility when those "articles" refer back to the company that publishes the newsletter. My friends at one of the largest trade publishing companies in the United States have told me repeatedly that they try for a **minimum** of a 60 – 40 ratio in all of their magazines. That means that between the covers of the magazine, at least 60 percent of the copy should be editorial content and no more than 40 percent advertising. Don't forget, that's the minimum, and if it's true for magazines, which are often meant to be read in a more leisurely fashion, the "editorial" percentage in a newsletter should be **MUCH** higher. People don't want ads in newsletters, and if they must appear, then keep them to a minimum. Additionally, readers don't want advertisement disguised as articles. Believe me, the public can be very dumb or very smart. When it comes to contrived stories, they know it.

Tom's Tip: In your newsletters, the editorial content should be a minimum of 80 percent or higher. I'd shoot for 90 to 95 percent.

Who cares? What's the tie-in with publicity? Well, an action-packed, information-filled newsletter performs the same duties of press releases and tip sheets. They give the media story ideas. You play the role of the source even if it's an indirect source. Here's an example. I know of one editor who receives a number of newsletters. I also know this editor uses the newsletters for potential stories, and he's even run the same article (or an expanded version) in his publication. He's also asked the writer of the newsletter to write articles for his publication.

I can't stress this enough: Journalists will keep, refer to and look forward to any source that provides them with good ideas for potential stories. You'll create an ambience of acceptance with your newsletter even if the stories emanating from it have nothing to do with the editor's needs. Guess who that editor will turn to when he needs someone with your background? An interesting group of short articles in a newsletter could easily find its way into the editor's "idea" folder I mentioned previously.

Also, let's get rid of this notion that a really "good-looking" newsletter matters. The best newsletters teem with information and are so relevant that you take the newsletter, punch holes in it and put it in a binder on your bookshelf or drop it into the idea folder.

And then you refer to it. That's the ultimate. One of the best no-frills, black-ink-on-white-paper newsletters, printed on one side and faxed to me, is the weekly newsletter by Adams Hudson. He's a terrific marketer, extremely smart and a superior wordsmith. Adams follows most of the rules that I suggest, and to his credit, he injects his personality – lots of southern charm and wit – in his newsletter, but NOT at the expense of content. If you want a sample copy of his fax newsletter, send him a fax at 334-262-1115 and ask for a sample. It's free, but be sure to tell him that Tom sent you.

Let me be blunt about newsletters. I still believe that tip sheets are the single best way to gain publicity through the media if done correctly and consistently. I would place newsletters that offer news-generating ideas and articles right behind tip sheets for effectiveness. Now that you know that, I also believe that most people are unwilling to offer solid news ideas in a newsletter. Take my forewarning to heart and don't commit the same sin.

Quick question: I've addressed a room full of public relations experts, and most will agree, their heads moving north and south in unison, that I'm dead right about the content of newsletters. Then why is it that these allegedly all-knowing professionals send out so many newsletters that break the rules by containing editorial content that is nothing more than advertising in disguise?

Why? Three reasons. First, it's that quirky human behavior pattern that we understand an issue intellectually but just can't put it into practice effectively. How many times have you read about how important it is to listen carefully, and how many times do you continue to interrupt someone when they're speaking? PR people often don't practice what they preach because the public relations person in them takes over from the newsperson that they should try to emulate.

Second, someone above the person editing the copy decides to send out a newsletter that is, in reality, nothing more than thinly disguised advertising (and unfortunately, often it's not even thinly disguised). The content goes out the window. They call this following the hand that writes the check. The boss or client, whomever is paying for the newsletter, insists that the newsletter become an excuse to brag rather than inform. The opposite of this, done with great subtlety and style, is the newsletter issued by York, Pa.-based The St. Onge Co., an internationally respected consulting firm providing strategic logistics services including supply chain optimization, distribution and manufacturing facility design, and operations planning and training. Their newsletter **only** discusses their clients' accomplishments. Of course, when you have dozens of Fortune 1,000 companies, it's impressive. What's more impressive is that St. Onge hasn't fallen into the trap of beating their own chest. The publicity value for them: their association with so many household names in American commerce. (Full Disclosure: St. Onge is a client. If you want a copy of their newsletter, contact me.)

The third reason that so many newsletters lack substance and effectiveness is that it takes *effort* to produce a regularly scheduled publication which shares relevant information. Mentioning the fact that you landed a big contract is strictly a "who cares?" news item for your clients and customers. If you're a jewelry retailer and mention that not only will you carry a new line of gem stones but that you'll be the exclusive distributor in the area and will sell them at a lower price than anyone in a 200-mile radius, that just might mean something. A newsletter that touts the 10 ways to spot phony diamonds means something. A newsletter to customers announcing your employee of the month just doesn't cut it. (However, praising employees in an internal, company newsletter is a fine idea and a great morale booster.)

Why are so many newsletters so dreadful? Effort and money. It takes more effort to provide interesting editorial content, especially if you intend to use fresh information that requires you to conduct the research and writing or hiring someone to do it. That translates into more costs. It's far easier and cheaper to use research that someone else has done than to conduct it yourself.

In the end, your newsletter must answer the "who cares?" question. If no one cares, don't include it. Send your news-carrying newsletter to your A, B and C list media contacts. Sooner or later they'll see the value and contact you for a story.

Tom's Tip: Ask yourself two questions for your external newsletter: 1) Who cares? And 2) Is it news?

If you **can't** answer these questions with clear, dispassionate clarity, then you should reassess your newsletter. If you lack the objectivity that's needed, ask the advice of someone who can. Newsletters can get you publicity. Just make sure it's news that you're sending out.

Chapter 12

The Op-Ed Page

An Obvious Outlet For Your Opinion

The Op-Ed page (opposite the editorial page) in a newspaper is the place where individuals can write opinion pieces about everything under the sun. (Most magazines don't have an Op-Ed page, but they sometimes use a hybrid of this type of article. Generally it falls under the category of guest columnist, guest editorial or something similar.) Its function mimics a newspaper except that the response time is much longer given magazines' deadlines. How important are Op-Ed pieces? Probably very few politicians with national ambitions aren't eager to have their Op-Ed piece appear in *The New York Times*.

People who regard themselves as cerebral, those who have a cause they want to publicize or someone who just feels they must vent publicly consider the Op-Ed page an important vehicle – especially for those engaged in public relations campaigns. Pick up your daily newspaper and turn to the editorial page, which will be on the left. The page on the opposite side, the right side, is the Op-Ed page. (Get it? Opposite the editorial page.) In some cases, all or part of that page might carry syndicated columnists. Most newspapers allow for outside contributors, though many newspapers prefer to use authors or topics with a local connection.

There are no guarantees that if you write an Op-Ed piece, the newspaper will publish it. But if you understand how to approach the task of writing an Op-Ed and follow my tips, you'll greatly increase the chances of seeing your opinion in print.

Those who obtain publicity through the Op-Ed page receive the coverage for a variety of reasons. There are rules you must follow if you hope to use this vehicle for publicity. Let's examine each.

Rule 1: Don't take it beyond the limit. In my first draft of this chapter, I wrote that good writing was the most important rule for appearing on the Op-Ed page. While revising this chapter, I placed it second for a very good reason. No matter how well written your article, no matter how colorful the language or successful your article is at inducing emotion, you must NOT exceed the word limit. It's like trying to put a window into a frame that's too small. It won't fit, and if the word length doesn't match, *most* editors won't use it. It's not complicated, yet I'm stunned at how frequently people submit pieces that are so long they simply don't have a prayer. True, the editor might consider shaving a few sentences if it only requires a slight slice – and that's a big maybe – but the simple truth is that the editor might not bother because he doesn't know what's really important (from the writer's perspective) and he might be just too lazy or indifferent to do the work. Invariably, when someone who is not a professional writer begins gushing about a topic or message that they feel needs airing, the tendency is to create a flood of words. Trust me, a trickle works better. What is the appropriate word length? The best way to find out is to call the daily newspapers on your media list and ask. If the list is too long (let's say you're considering sending your Op-Ed piece to the top 100 newspapers in the United States), then stay within the range of 650 to 800 words. Believe me, shorter is better. A tight, well-written 650-word piece has a much better chance than one at 790 words. You might not think that those additional 140 words matter, but they do. The only commodity newspapers have is the paper on which things are printed. It's also one of their largest expenses. To newspapers and editors, paper and the space on that paper are precious indeed.

Also, you must understand that the larger national newspapers consider an Op-Ed piece **only** if they have exclusivity. If lightning strikes and *The New York Times* and *The Wall Street Journal* both publish your opinion piece, it is unlikely they will use you in the future. Indeed, they often insist on exclusivity. But this is mainly true of the top 10 or 20 American newspapers. This is usually untrue of smaller newspapers. They probably won't check or care. If you're going to distribute your Op-Ed piece to the top 20, it might pay to find out what policy they follow for simultaneous submissions of opinion pieces. For the rest of the newspapers, I would just submit it.

Rule 2: Golden words rule the world of words.

"Who called love conquering,
When its sweet flower
So easily dries among the sour
Languages of the living?"

Beautiful, isn't it? The words are from the poem, "Who Called Love Conquering" by the late, beloved English poet, Philip Larkin. For most people who read Larkin's few words, it touches you a bit even if you don't quite know what he means. Somehow the words make you feel *something*. The same holds true for writing an Op-Ed piece. Simply put, the better your writing, the greater the chance that the newspaper will publish your Op-Ed article. That means your language, style, rules of grammar and the ability to express coherent thought must be enticing to a person who, as part of his job, reads a great deal every day. It must be a compelling read whenever possible. It's also vital that you have someone proofread your work. Be sure that proofreader is competent in the English language and edits your article ruthlessly. It must be free of clichés, spelling or grammatical errors. Presuming that English is your primary language, don't send in an Op-Ed piece that's so poorly written the editor reading it will snicker and say: "Obviously, English isn't his first language. I wonder what his first language is." This isn't a joke. I've heard editors say this. I've said this about articles that have crossed my desk. (I'm sure people have said it about me.)

Rule 3: Have something to say. Go back to our definition of news. Again, the goal is to provide information that is "*relevant* to people's lives, *useful* to them or *interesting*." [my emphasis] If you're too shrill or self-serving or if your article is a thinly disguised attempt at blatant publicity, you'll have trouble getting your article accepted. Just ask yourself that perennial question: Is my opinion on this topic relevant, useful or interesting to people's lives?

Rule 4: Don't be shy about your expertise. Do tout your expertise with as powerful a hand as you can wield. But don't proudly pound your chest by overtly promoting yourself in the article. When you write an Op-Ed piece, you can use the tagline for self-promotion. The tagline is the paragraph at the end of the article that describes who you are. Implicit in this description is a mention of your expertise. For example, if I write an Op-Ed piece on the topic of publicity and its effectiveness for not-for-profits, here are two versions I might use: T.S. Peric' is the president of Galileo Communications Inc. and the author of *Wacky Days: How to Get Millions of $$$ in Free Publicity By Creating a "Real" Holiday & Other Tactics Used by Media Experts.* You can contact him at tom@wackydays.com.

Better yet: T.S. Peric', president of Cherry Hill, NJ-based Galileo Communications Inc., is the author of *Wacky Days: How to Get Millions of $$$ in Free Publicity By Creating a "Real" Holiday & Other Tactics Used by Media Experts.* He frequently consults on publicity issues with not-for-profits and can be reached at tom@wackydays.com. Transparent, screeching, self-promotion? I think not. Did my tagline clearly identify who I am and what qualifications I had to write the article? Yes.

Rule 5: What really works for? Being the first person to address a topic or providing a fresh slant on an existing topic grabs readers' and editors' attention and greatly increases your chances of the newspaper publishing your Op-Ed piece.

Taking a contrarian view is also a good rule. Just be sure that you believe in the contrarian view you're espousing or you could regret it later. (Once printed, it becomes a matter of record.)

Here's an example. Let's pretend you're a psychologist. You would like more publicity and decide to write an Op-Ed piece in the wake of a murder trial that has occurred in your hometown. Not surprisingly, the media showcases the trial on a daily basis, with some psychological experts disagreeing on whether the defendant is sane or insane. In an offhand conversation, you hear local residents grumbling that the insanity plea will probably get the defendant off. You know, however, that despite the notoriety and attention given to the insanity plea, it is successful in less than one percent of criminal cases when the defense uses it. As they say, "Think about that." You, the psychologist and the expert, write the Op-Ed piece, explaining that this type of plea is almost always unsuccessful and juries in an overwhelming majority of cases find the defendant guilty.

Timeliness is critical to submitting an Op-Ed piece. If your view is too late, editors will consider it old news. Is there a magic time limit? No, because each newspaper editor has his own built-in sundial for judging time. If you wait longer than two weeks, I would suggest that you're beginning to push the boundary. Every day that you wait to submit your Op-Ed article, you're increasing the odds against someone publishing it if your opinion deals with an event in the recent past. I represent a division of a major American utility company whose stock trades on the New

York Stock Exchange. This division was new and needed some local coverage in the area where they employed contractors in the heating, air conditioning and ventilation business. One Monday, I received a concerned call from my client because *Dateline NBC*, a national TV show, had aired an investigation into the tactics of unscrupulous contractors in Houston. This was a national story with implicit charges that tainted contractors everywhere. My client understood this. You should be thinking the same way. We obtained a transcript of the TV show and immediately responded in a local newspaper with an Op-Ed piece. They not only published our opinion, they ran a photo of my client. Except for national newspapers such as *The New York Times*, *The Wall Street Journal* or *The Washington Post*, local coverage prevails over regional or national. That is, the more your opinion directly affects the readership of your newspaper (or magazine), the more likely you are to have your Op-Ed piece published. We did this with our defense of the *local* contracting industry. While the investigation focused on Houston, we made the information relevant to readership in the area where my client operates.

As I write this chapter, in today's *Philadelphia Inquirer* is an opinion piece by Katherine Ramsland. Her article raises doubt that Albert DeSalvo was the infamous Boston strangler. Her tagline? "Katherine Ramsland teaches forensic psychology at DeSales University [a local school]. Her latest book is "*The Forensic Science of C.S.I.*"

Ms. Ramsland saw the connection between her topic and her book. Book writers will often write an Op-Ed piece to tout their book, and that's just fine because it makes good publicity sense. Ms. Ramsland had the added cachet of being a teacher at a local university.

Indeed, just being a reader (and presumably a resident) of the area helps get you published. Here's where the issue of a local connection and timing matters. I once submitted a piece on the subject of the penetration of British Intelligence by the Soviet Union. It was tied to a book that had been written earlier, but the audience – a major Midwest city – didn't have a natural tie-in to the topic. The editors chose to use it, I suspect, because the writing was crisp and clear (all modesty aside) and because I mentioned that I was in graduate school studying International Affairs (establishing my modest expertise). I'm quite sure that mentioning I was a former resident of the city helped. If even one element had been missing, I'm not sure that they would have published my article.

A True Story: Someone in my hometown read this article, called my father in California, faxed him the piece and told him he had a smart son. The assessment might have been wrong, but it was nice to hear my father so pleased when he called to congratulate me. Why did I write this piece? It certainly had nothing to do with publicity. I wrote it because I felt like it. Plus, the piece garnered the attention of someone important to me: my dad.

Rule 6: Don't badger the newspaper after you've had some success. Most newspapers have an "unofficial" number of appearances in a year in which they will print an Op-Ed article by the same writer. They might not have this number published or even formalized; but informally they probably work under the premise that two to four times per year is plenty. If you've had a few successes, give the editor an opportunity to breathe before submitting another Op-Ed piece. I would suggest, without knowing the individual policy of your newspaper, that a maximum of four Op-Ed pieces annually is about right. If you've had an Op-Ed piece published, call the editor of the editorial page and ask if they have a limit. Don't guess. It's not difficult. Just pick up the telephone or send an e-mail and ask.

Rule 7: Take a dose of reality. As in most things, you must base your likelihood of success on the quality of what you produce (your writing), timing, luck and the competition. For Op-Ed pieces, that means if you write it well, in most instances you have a good chance. The Op-Ed piece is popular with publicity hounds because with a little planning it is not that difficult to get one published. However, if you want to appear in the pages of one of my favorite newspapers, *The Wall Street Journal*, you're going to have very tough sledding. The competition is fierce. How many submissions do you think *The Wall Street Journal* receives every day? I'm sure it's at least 100. If you discount the obvious – if you're a head of state, you'll get in – that means they might use one to three per day. Maybe. Don't be discouraged. At most magazines and daily newspapers you'll have very good chances.

Remember the most important rule: Keep submitting. After all, everyone is entitled to your opinion.

Chapter 13

The Letter

"Dear Somebody . . ."

"My baby, she wrote me a letter,"
from *The Letter* by The Box Tops

As I write this, a director of a company I represent called me to say thanks for obtaining 25 issues of a special supplement to a trade magazine that covers his industry. He thought the supplement so informative that he planned on using it in his training program. (By now you've read all these stories of mine and are probably thinking, if you have an overabundance of suspicious genes, that I'm making them up or embellishing them. I swear they are true. Strap me to the lie detector.)

Ever the publicity guy, I accepted his thanks but immediately suggested we write to the parent magazine that sponsored the supplement and offer our thanks. To ensure that the editor would publish our letter, I suggested that we mention the practical usage of the supplement. Naturally, my client's signature and company affiliation at the end of the letter to the editor would identify him as the author. Commenting positively on the special supplement, which is frequently a creation of the advertising department, would go over well with the magazine. Our letter would serve as a reinforcement vehicle to the magazine's readers that the publication was doing a fine job. We simply praised the article in the supplement and said it was helpful to us. It was "signed" by the client and included his title and company name. We made it into print. It was an undemanding approach that worked.

Letters to a publication, a newspaper or magazine, through a channel called "letter to the editor", can be a sure-fire way to obtain publicity. A letter to the editor is a cousin to an Op-Ed page article. That's not a bad way of thinking about how to write your letter to the editor. Write it as though you're writing directly to one person. Letters to the editor generally address a topic that the publication has already covered or raises an issue about a topic it should cover.

Indeed, commenting on a topic and agreeing or disagreeing with it publicly is a good approach in a letter to the editor. Sometimes writers use letters to compliment or scold a journalist. Other times they use them to add more information that didn't appear in the original article or to point out something the writer missed.

The basics still apply here. Show why a common practice or idea is wrong or why someone (the newspaper, for example) might have missed an aspect to a story they covered. Letters to the editor (and Op-Ed) pieces tend to have a greater chance of success if they take a contrarian viewpoint. The big difference between the Op-Ed page article and the letter to the editor is that an Op-Ed piece often calls for some type of expertise, even if it's implicit. The letter to the editor is from Joe and Josephine Average sharing their opinion. Nothing more. Again, use clean, simple, short sentences with uncomplicated thoughts and you can't go wrong. You must be able to write with some clarity, of course, and you should not use the letter to the editor forum only to vent or lie. A passionate, rousing letter can be a real plus in increasing your chance of publication, especially if you keep it short. Editors love short stuff, even if most people aren't capable of delivering a message succinctly. I would suggest a length of 100 to 300 words maximum. (There are approximately 250 words to a double-spaced, typewritten page.) That's why publications always run that disclaimer stating that they (the editors) have the right to edit and shorten your writing. It's not a conspiracy, though many people outside the business believe it is. It's just that some of what comes across the editor's desk appears to be the ranting of a disheveled brain in torment who insists upon his own rules of grammar, punctuation and clarity. Most newspapers will print your name and the city where you live or work. Many magazines will publish the title and name of your company.

Tom's Tip: Whenever possible without using a bludgeon, to gain name recognition (publicity) and to establish your expertise. For example, let's say that your daily newspaper prints an article about which restaurants have failed sanitary inspections. You just opened a restaurant and need some publicity. You write a letter explaining how your 10-step cleanliness guide is mandatory reading for each employee and that you post it in all work areas and even in the bathroom. In that letter you mention that: 1) "As a restaurateur for 17 years . . . 2) At my newly opened Heavenly Divine Restaurant on Market Street, all employees are required to read and sign a copy of . . . 3) If any other restaurants want copies of the guide, I'll be happy to provide them free of charge." Newspapers will publish this kind of letter provided you actually offer information that informs, entertains or is relevant to their readers. Also, be sure to include an address AND daytime telephone number. The newspaper will call you to verify that you actually wrote the letter so that you can't write a vindictive piece and sign your ex-wife's name to it.

Take It To the Limit? Is there a limit to the number of letters to the editor that you can write? The same rule for frequency of submissions applies to letters to the editor as it does to Op-Ed articles. You can probably assume (yes, I know that's a dangerous word) that most newspapers will publish a letter from a reader two to four times a year, a magazine once or twice a year. If this isn't enough for you, just call the publication and ask.

Try this test and let me know what happens (Tom@wackydays.com). Call your favorite magazine or local newspaper and ask for the editor who handles the letters to the editor section. (I'll bet you they fumble this question almost immediately because there really isn't one person in charge.) Then ask how many letters (or Op-Ed pieces) they accept from one person in a given year. I'd be astonished if they have a firm number. What they'll probably tell you is that it depends on the article or letter: how well-written, its relevance, etc. What that really means is somewhere between two and four times each year. With computerization, it's even a bit harder to "sneak" in more frequently because editors can quickly search the archives to see how often the person submits Op-Ed articles or letters to the editor.

Tom's Tip: Here's my advice. Everyone should write two letters to the editor and two Op-Ed pieces every year. That's one piece per quarter. Sure, it's a gamble in time and effort, but you should be writing one if for no other reason than because you're a concerned citizen. If you can't think of any topics, I'd suggest that you reconsider your creative I. Q. Keep in mind that on the Op-Ed side, you're the expert so bring your expertise directly into play. The letter to the editor can be from the heart. It just doesn't hurt that you're an expert, too. Keep your article or letter short and write it tight and bright. And don't forget the basic rule of most letters. You're writing to one person. In this case, it's the editor. Make it as compelling as possible and you stand a very good chance of seeing it in print.

Chapter 14

Signing Up For The Editorial Board

The Board Walk

Many publications, especially magazines in the trade press, have an editorial board. You find it on or near the masthead that lists the persons responsible for the publication, like the publisher and editor. The editorial board serves several purposes. Magazines use it to gain credibility in the industry they cover. They choose people (and their companies in the process) who often have a perceived expertise or reputation in the industry. This allows the magazine to boast, in essence, that the publication is serious and knowledgeable about the industry it covers. What do you get from being on the editorial board? You get to say: "I'm on the editorial board, with all the other experts. This magazine thinks so much of me, they asked me (and my company's name) to be listed in this publication." Publicity-minded people use the editorial board as a repetitive, easy and highly visible way of informing people inside and outside the industry that they're experts. After all, that's why the magazine put them on the editorial board.

What are the duties of an editorial board member? They range from doing nothing to examining a few stories from the magazine each year and possibly contributing an article or your view on various articles (editorial content).

In short, the duties are usually very light or nonexistent. It doesn't hurt having your name on the masthead every month for your term. (Terms vary, but most editorial board members serve for at least one year; often it runs into several years. Each magazine has its own policy.) Editorial boards are one of the best-kept secrets in the publicity business. I've always been amazed at how relatively easy it is to get on an editorial board. It usually requires three things: 1) You should be knowledgeable about the industry. You don't have to be an expert, but if you've been in the applicable business for a decade, I could get you to qualify; 2) You have to ask. Most people never get on an editorial board because they fail to ask; 3) You must follow through with your request. If a certain magazine holds particular appeal, but they just reconfigured their board, which lasts for two years, you must renew your request in 18 months (six months before they reconfigure it again). In other words, think strategically.

Tom's Tip: ? Again, **you ask**. I usually write to the publisher of the magazine. The publisher is the head of a publication (think president) and is in charge of the business end. He has the last word on editorial content, though editors make most of the day-to-day decisions. It's fair to say that the publisher almost always has some input on the editorial board. The editor might or might not. In this case, start at the top with your request. Some publishers link a listing on the editorial board masthead to advertising in the magazine. **Don't**. This book is about free publicity, not about paying for it. If the publisher makes any suggestions about advertising and links it to the editorial board, walk away unless you really want to spend money. I would go to this magazine's competitor and try to get on that editorial board. Also, it's rare that you can be on the editorial board of competing magazines in an industry. So choose a pecking order of magazines and start at the top of the list.

Be smart. When you approach the publisher, be sure you're a subscriber, and start that subscription as early as possible before making your request. Then write a letter to the publisher asking to be on the board. Tell him how much you like the magazine, how you've been a loyal subscriber, and describe your background. Mention that you would be an active board member (even though you probably won't have to be) and offer your assistance in any way possible. Now, the reason you're on the subscription list is that if the publisher decides to check, he can actually verify that you're familiar with the magazine because you subscribe rather than someone who is simply sucking up to get on the editorial board.

Is being on an editorial board worth the effort? Well, what's it worth to appear every month, sometimes for years, in a publication that you decided is important for publicity? Plus, you get to add that monthly mention on your resume or bio . . . Joe Smith is on the editorial board of . . . magazine. And what's it worth in terms of publicity when the cost to you is ZERO? Using an editorial board takes minimum effort but is a strategic publicity move. It is also an extremely effective way to promote your name in a specific industry. All you have to do is take a walk along the boardwalk and ask.

A few thoughts about boards (and the advice they offer).

Once you've given advice to someone, you're obligated.
Malcolm Forbes, publisher

Advice is more agreeable in the mouth than in the ear.
Mason Cooley, U.S. aphorist

Chapter 15

Create Your Own Holidays

Wacky Days (And Ways) For Publicity

I own the Web site www.wackydays.com and the toll free number 1-877-wackydays (for phone orders only). I even created my own holiday. I named it "Publicity For Profit Week." If that doesn't convince you that I believe in creating days (or weeks and months) around which to wrap a publicity effort, I don't know what else to do. If anything in American business expresses the freedom to do as you wish while pursuing your financial dreams, it must be the ability to create an event of any type in this country and then promote it. You can even create your own holiday.

Creating an event is, in essence, going for the knockout in terms of publicity. You marshal all your energy in order to gain all possible attention during a specific time frame: day, week or month. It's a marvelous approach because it forces you to focus your attention on one climactic moment for which you created the event. The downside, of course, is that if you fail, all your effort goes down the drain. Kinda. Let me explain.

Essentially, you can create two types of events: a one-shot event that you won't repeat and an event that might gain the benefit of repeat coverage. Naturally, the latter makes the most sense because you've already spent your opportunity costs – that initial, overwhelming effort – and you don't have to start from scratch each time.

Let's start with one-time events. This type of publicity effort often centers on some action which captures the media's attention because of what you do or what you say you intend to do. The most common, one-time event is probably a grand opening of a single location (by definition, a one-time event). You can never have another one (though I've seen a few people make a lame attempt at it). Pretend that you have a new doughnut shop, and you want to gain as much attention as possible. What should you do? This is a big order for publicity because who cares whether another doughnut shop opens?

But a doughnut shop in Colorado that obtained advice from a public relations firm did a pretty good job of making this opening original. In fact, it delivered a knockout. It teamed up with the local police department and had a doughnut-tasting contest. Because there's always been a somewhat humorous stereotype of overweight police officers munching doughnuts endlessly, the department made sure it sent only fit-looking officers to the event. The doughnut shop promised to donate 10 percent of all the income from the first day to the local police fund. This event was an overwhelming success, gaining local television and newspaper coverage. That initial rush of new customers can literally make or break a retail business. By hyping this new enterprise, they passed that critical first hurdle: creating an initial list of loyal customers.

Tom's Tip: If you're going to conduct a one-time event, be sure to send out the requisite press release before the event. Follow up with phone calls, especially if you have a hook like the Colorado doughnut shop. On the day of the event, send out a media alert. This is a one-page sheet that answers these basic questions: Who, What, When, Where, Why and sometimes How. (For a sample media alert, turn to the Appendix.) Be sure to give the media some urgent reason to cover your event. This one-page information sheet is both a tease and a bare essentials summary. (If you're faxing it on the day of the event, you might want to send it to *two* people in the newsroom to reduce the chances that your target person doesn't act because they never got it.)

The Real Secret To "Creating" An Event. By now you realize that my favorite approach in publicity is to set in motion a system where the basics repeat themselves, and you don't start from scratch each time: You reap the benefits from the first-time effort. Nothing could be a better example of this than creating an event. The "real" secret is that you take your event and tie it to a holiday that already exists or which you literally create by yourself. Let's examine both.

Celebrating with an existing event. What is an existing event or holiday? A little background. You've certainly heard of Arbor Day, Breast Cancer Awareness Month, Black History Month, etc. Are you familiar with National Epitaph Day or International Quality of Life Month? Probably not. I bet plenty of disc jockeys "know" that Feb. 6th is the anniversary of the Beatles' first visit to America or that Feb. 8 is Laugh and Get Rich Day.

How do media people know this? It's the pre-Internet secret of journalists, libraries, researchers and the like: *Chase's Calendar of Events*. Virtually every library has a reference copy. The calendar started in 1957 when the Chase brothers – Bill and Harrison – created a list of various events in a 32-page "book". It didn't have an entry for every single day of the year, but it became popular because the brothers created it in response to requests by journalists who were always on the lookout for a feature story.

They added to their growing list when they took over the U.S. Department of Commerce's "Special Days, Weeks and Months," which comprised a list of events compiled by trade associations. *Chase's* was on its way. You can now buy the annual *Chase's* volume for about $59.

According to *Chase's*, "Chase's Calendar of Events contains more than 12,000 entries and is over 700 pages long. We limit entries to those that are of national or broadly regional interest, or those that seem to have some special entertainment value. Sponsors of events are not charged for inclusion in the calendar."(I love *Chase's* because while the price of many directories can run into the hundreds of dollars, this one is still affordable for most people and accessible free to everyone via the library.)

You can wrap your publicity activity around an event that already exists by virtue of its listing in *Chase's*. Just draw a connection between the event and your own publicity goal. For example, if you're an air-conditioning contractor, it makes sense to create a tie-in with the 100th anniversary of the discovery of air conditioning and which *Chase's* lists in its directory. Just tie your publicity efforts to a celebration that exists (such as our 100th anniversary example) and issue a press release or begin a media campaign.

Celebrating With An Event You Create.

But there's even a better way, and it takes virtually no effort. **You can "create" your own holiday, register it and, if you wish, promote it ruthlessly.** Here's how.

It's true that many of the events in both *Chase's* and John Kremer's book, *Celebrate Today* (another directory of holidays, anniversaries etc.), can be considered wacky, unusual, a bit funny, if off the wall. Some of these holidays clearly demonstrate a profit motive behind the creator. However, many have a serious purpose, often educating people in the attempt to create a better world in which to live. Also remember that some days of celebration become not only huge but also accepted by most Americans.

Here's a light-hearted example of a holiday that garners media attention every year. It's Plan Your Epitaph Day, on Nov. 2. I interviewed Lance Hardie, the founder of this "holiday", years ago when I worked as the editor of one of the nation's largest small-business magazines. Hardie started this annual event urging people to write their own epitaph. For a nominal fee, he'll write one for you. I interviewed Hardie again for this book, and he confirmed that interviews with journalists (especially radio) pick up as his special day draws near. Each year, he'll start doing radio interviews as journalists look in the calendar for something interesting. Indeed, because *Chase's* lists his event, all Hardie has to do is sit back and wait for the media to come to him. That's how I found him. Nice guy, too. (www.hardiehouse.org/epitaph)

But the best recent example of this type of promotion is Kwanzaa, which Maulana Karenga, a black-studies professor at the University of California (Long Beach), created as a nonreligious holiday that highlights family and social values for African-Americans. By the early 1990s, an estimated 5 million people celebrated this holiday. Clearly, his idea, promoted by the media, made this holiday a mainstream event. Today, no media outlet would ignore this holiday any more than they would either Christmas or Hanukkah.

You can gear your special promotion around an existing event or create your own and send it to *Chase's*. You can register with *Chase's* at www.chases.com or go to the library, ask for a copy and photocopy the last page of the book, which has an application form. **Keep in mind that this is FREE!** Another book that celebrates various days and events is John Kremer's *Celebrate Today*, which he updates yearly with a CD-ROM. A listing in *Celebrate Today* is also free.

In an exclusive interview with ***Wacky Days***, Kremer answered these questions.

1) ***Wacky Days*:** How can people create their own "day" and get included in your CD? The book I bought has a copyright of 1995, so I'm assuming (dangerous word, I know) that you haven't issued an update. I suspect the updates come through the CDs.

John Kremer: "Updates do come on the CD – up to 15,500 events."

2) ***Wacky Days:*** What is the best way for readers to approach you for inclusion into your CD and book? What must they do?

John Kremer: "The procedure for applying is simply to e-mail me (johnkremer@bookmarket.com) the complete info on the day. Then I will enter it into the database. The database will soon be available online for a small subscription fee as well as in a variety of targeted books and calendars."

3) ***Wacky Days:*** What are the most common reasons you DO NOT include someone's homemade celebration day?

John Kremer: "It duplicates an event already being celebrated. It's too local, not of national or international interest. It's not clearly defined. It has a terrible name – too awkward, flat or boring, or is unclear. I rarely reject a day."

Tom's Tip: A few closing reminders. If you're going to "create" a day, register both with *Chase's* and John Kremer.

Also, think long term. What might start as a fun publicity idea can evolve into a real fireball of activity and publicity when handled correctly. Keep in mind Lance Hardie's low-key approach, the stunning acceptance of Kwanzaa and the marvelous good done for women with Breast Cancer Awareness Month.

Tom's Tip: Guess what's the No. 1 reason that *Chase's* drops listings in its calendar? After you gain entry into the calendar, you MUST renew your entry annually. All you do is fill out a simple form. A spokeswoman at *Chase's* told me that about 30 percent of the entrants fail to renew their information each year, forcing the publication to remove their entry from the calendar.

Chapter 16

Getting On The List

Making It Automatic

During my seminars, people usually ask what I think are the most effective ways to get free publicity. They ask me: "Is there one secret formula or magic approach (if there were, wouldn't we all employ it?) that would guarantee media coverage?" They are often a bit surprised at my answer. I tell them that while there are no guarantees for getting publicity, getting your name or organization on a "permanent" listing in a publication is about as close as you can come to a guaranteed approach if you fit the criteria. I'm always amazed that most people ignore this one method of obtaining media attention, which is free and often repetitive in nature. Let me explain. Go through your local newspaper and you'll see several if not a dozen (depending on where you live) different outlets for free publicity.

Publications have essentially two types of lists or postings. The first type, which I call the temporary event, changes with each issue of the publication. These sections allow you to mention a class, lecture or promotion for a one-time event (of short duration) that involves you or your company. Let's say you want to give a lecture about how to develop better study habits, and the location is your local high school. You decide that the "Our Town" section is the ideal place for this posting or placement and send the information to the appropriate editor. (Hopefully, you also sent a press release to the city editor because you might just stir up a news or feature story about your class.) You get a one-time mention in your local newspaper, and that's the end of the promotion. Maybe it brought in a few more students. The end of the event curtails any more mentions in the media.

The other types of lists are almost permanent because the basic information seldom changes, yet they appear on a regular basis. I call them merry-go-round listings. For example, your newspaper might list (as mine does) information about a local science museum that focuses on children. Besides identifying the museum, it includes location, exhibits, hours of operation, etc. What I love about these lists is that once you're in, it's usually permanent as long as you respond to the periodic inquiries about whether the information is correct. It's a matter of providing a "yes" update to the media outlet. There are virtually dozens of these print outlets in major cities, from giveaways to weekly magazines and newspapers to the largest daily newspaper or local business publication. This is also becoming true of Internet postings and listings and public access (cable) television.

Tom's Tip: I would spend at least one afternoon (two if you're a national company with customers from across the United States) to see where you could post events and meetings in a "listing" or "posting" section of various newspapers or magazines. I would also spend at least one afternoon (do it on a weekend when it's raining or snowing) and search the Internet for free postings. Be sure that your business is included in any posting of a national membership directory, especially if you serve a specific territory. For example, if you're an HVACR contractor, make sure that someone can find you by various geographic searches if they need a contractor. I'm a member of Toastmasters in my town, and we have postings in several publications which draw potential members. We are discovering – no surprise here – that most people visit us via information gleaned from the Internet. The beauty of lists and Internet postings is that you conduct the "heavy lifting," the searching for an appropriate, free posting, once a year and then only need to spend minimal if any time keeping it up-to-date.

Tom's Tip: Ever wonder what criteria editors use to decide who to include or exclude from their lists? First, the rules vary according to every publication or broadcast media. The key to being included for an event is often: 1) Whether it is open to the public; 2) Whether it's free or there's a minimal charge; 3) Whether it has a charitable or educational component or benefit to the attendees. These events have a high probability of getting into the media. Let's return to our previously mentioned study course. If you're charging no fee or only $5 per student, you'll probably get a mention. If your seminar is for the bar exam (thus taking it out of the mainstream) and the charge is $100, the newspaper will probably not publish a mention of your course (though they might suggest that you buy an advertisement). This approach is exactly the REVERSE for trade publications. Trade publications usually don't want the general public involved but rather seek people in the specific industry covered by the magazine. If they're offering a refresher course on air conditioning and it's sponsored by *Contracting Business* magazine, you had better be in the HVACR industry if you plan on signing up. They aren't interested in you, as a member of the public, attending if you only want to fix the air conditioner in junior's room.

Be sure to **ALWAYS** send out a press release for basic events, promotions, new hires, and new store openings to the media. This should be as automatic as coffee, tea or Coca Cola in the morning. Every company should send a press release and a photo for every person the company promotes.

Let me end with a final example. One of my three local daily newspapers has a section entitled "How to Contact Monday Business." Under that headline, it offers contact information for sections of this newspaper that appear on a regular basis (usually weekly). This includes:

- People in the News (brief items about promotions, appointments and new hires).
- Business Calendar (business-related meetings, programs and seminars).
- On the Commercial Front (brief items on commercial property leases or sales).
- On the Boards (Items about new appointments to the board of directors of corporations or nonprofit organizations).
- Ideas for local business stories.

My local newspaper makes it easy. Whether the local newspaper prints a contact list for you or you must do a little digging, it is not difficult to obtain concrete results by getting your name in the listings or postings of newspapers and magazines. All you have to do is create the list and follow through. It's an effective, low-effort approach to publicity that should become automatic.

It's free, it's easy, and it's often repetitive. It's a marvel to me that more people don't do it, and I really don't know why. Spend a small amount of time, and wherever you can get a free posting about you, your business or organization, take advantage of it. Keep your eyes open for these free yet powerful postings. While it may not have great readership each time, how many readers scan those postings over several months or even a year? A lot. It's publicity, it's free, so use it.

Chapter 17

Contests

And The Winner Is . . .

Sponsoring a contest is another way to obtain free publicity. There are only three limitations to using contests for your publicity goals. The first and most powerful limitation is your imagination. With creativity, effort and suggestions from friends and people you trust, this is a limitation that is fun and rewarding when you overcome it. The other two limitations are a time commitment needed to run a contest and the money or value of the prize that you're offering. You can have contests based on skill, luck or a combination of both. The common thread, of course, is how will the contest draw media attention and what connection does the contest have to your product, service or organization.

Let's use a fairly easy example. Some independently owned bookstores are suffering because of the Internet. It appears that those which continue to operate profitably fit well into their community and offer much more than "just books." It can be a café attached to your bookstore, book readings or writers' classes. You might decide the children's market is a great source of revenue (for children's books and the parents that visit because of their kids) so you sponsor a "Name the Children's Section" contest. You offer to name that part of the store from the names submitted by children from three local elementary schools in your town. First, you contact the principal of each school and ask if their fourth-graders would like to participate. If even one classroom cooperates, you're in business. It helps to mention that you might have some media coverage and would like the winner to come to a special event at the bookstore on Saturday morning for the award (a nonschool day naturally and in time for the Sunday newspaper, which generally has the highest circulation). After issuing the press release, choose the room name that wins the contest. If you feel comfortable with adding several people as judges, that's an even better way of proving how "above board" your contest is. (Don't forget to issue a press release AFTER you've chosen a name, with a photo of the winner. That's winning the publicity game on both ends.)

Tom's Tip: Don't limit media involvement with your contest by only trying to get press coverage. Ask a journalist to be a judge. If I owned a restaurant and had a cooking contest, I'd certainly try to get the local food critic(s) to serve as a judge. The same rule applies to art, theater and so on. We have a local bureau of the *Philadelphia Inquirer* in New Jersey (naturally, the main office is across the river, 20 minutes away in Philadelphia). If I ran the contest to name the children's section of the bookstore, you can bet I'd call the bureau chief and ask him to be a judge. Unless there's a company prohibition against being a judge, what answer do you think you'll receive? If the bureau chief accepts, do you think he just MIGHT assign the contest as a news story? Also, if the contest has some real competitive aspects to it (a writing contest, for example), then public scrutiny helps not only to legitimize the contest but makes it more likely that the media will consider it a public service to promote rather than a cheap publicity stunt. If you can enlist a media outlet as one of the sponsors of the event, you've really hit a home run. The media doesn't like to be used, nor is it likely that they will promote your business simply so that you can make more money. If your contest has charitable or educational overtones or if you're a not-for-profit, you have a much better chance. The criteria used by the media for contests vary, but these are the questions they will think about: Is it open to the public? How interesting or challenging is the contest? Who are the potential participants? The more open and interesting (or challenging) it is, the more likely the media will cover your contest. The media will probably not hype a contest in a company with 25 employees that is restricted to the workers.

One final point on sponsoring contests. Try to choose a contest that becomes an annual affair. Make it repetitive. I harp on this point, and, yes, it can be a great deal of work the first time you do it. But by holding the contest annually, you've already paid the opportunity costs in the initial effort (and attempts at publicity). After that, your contest could very well fit into the calendar of events that the local newspaper or magazine covers. Don't reinvent the wheel. If I'm in your town, I'll be happy to volunteer as a judge. A well-thought-out, interesting, annual contest can be a sure-fire winner in gaining publicity for you, year after year.

And that keeps you in the publicity winner's circle.

A few thoughts about contests.

We improve ourselves by victories over ourself. There must be contests, and you must win.
Edward Gibbon, historian

Maybe a nation that consumes as much booze and dope as we do and has our kind of divorce statistics should pipe down about "character issues." Either that or just go ahead and determine the presidency with three-legged races and pie-eating contests. It would make better TV.
P.J. O'Rourke, American writer

Chapter 18

Giving An Award

"I Would Like To Thank The Academy . . ."

I like the idea of giving an Academy Award acceptance speech. It seems like fun going up to a lectern and gushing about how you love many of the people you probably hate. Giving (or receiving) an award can be as effective as creating a contest for gaining publicity. The major difference is that I consider giving an award a shortcut to getting media attention – it is usually far less time-consuming than a contest and lacks its potential for failure because you don't have enough contestants or can't generate sufficient interest. Who doesn't like receiving an award? I received a psuedo-award for earning my Competent Toastmaster (CTM) award in only nine months. A fellow toastmaster wanted to give a speech from an advanced manual which required her to give an award. She created the Roadrunner Award and presented it to me for the rapid speed at which I blazed through 10 speeches. (In Toastmasters, the CTM is the basic speaking award. To earn it, you must give 10 speeches, each on dissimilar topics and with a different goal.) Even though this award was make-believe, the accomplishment was real life. I enjoyed the award, which consisted of a Pez candy dispenser featuring Wile E. Coyote and the Roadrunner. (My son liked it even more.) My point is that it was fun getting this award even if it wasn't *real*. Let's be honest. Who doesn't like getting an award, especially when the recipient earns it based on some real accomplishment? I still crow (in a quiet way) about winning a national journalism scholarship (among others) for college, which saved me thousands of dollars. Why did I hang plaques in my office depicting several journalism awards? Why do you think there's such a market for bowling and baseball trophies? It makes us feel good, it reaffirms our skills and knowledge and it displays our accomplishments to others. And the best awards can be those that come out of the blue, the ones for which we've never entered or applied.

The point of all this is that if you give an award, it has a reasonable chance of making its way into your local newspaper or magazine, even if it amounts to only a paragraph or two. If the award is grand enough, or the setting for presenting the award impressive enough, or the presenter of the award is a personality or local celebrity, you just might get real news coverage from your local media. You can almost guarantee media coverage for an award if you present it to a media outlet. Common sense should prevail here. Here's an example. When I was in charge of communications for tourism in a major Midwest city, we always gave an award to a journalist for his coverage of this town as a destination city. During my tenure, we gave the award to a television journalist during National Tourism Week. Do you think the person receiving the award showed up during the presentation? Of course. They usually showed up with a camera crew. Guess who won the award the previous year? If my memory is correct, if you guessed a competing television station, you would be right. Get the picture? (I had nothing to do with this award process but had to chuckle a bit during my analysis of it.) If you're the sole arbiter of who wins based, of course, on some subjective criteria through which you can ram a truck filled with potential reasoning (to protect you from any criticism), you've got a winner. After all, you've picked the winner, and if the media carries the award event, you or your product, service or company wins, too. (Ever wonder why some television station staffers, usually in the newsroom, seem to be the recipient of so many awards?) It demonstrates an organization or business combining idealism (presumably the media outlet did something worthy even if it was part of the job) with practicality and publicity sense.

Tom's Tip: If you already have an annual function that you attend because you created the event or help sponsor it, or if it is part of your industry, think about how you can add an award that raises your visibility. If the award involves the media, so much the better. (Members of the media can either be winners of the award or judges.)

Here's an example. Let's say you're new in the financial planning business and you want to make your presence known quickly. You don't have the time or inclination to wait five years before people know who you are. You sit down and realize that in a few months your professional association's annual trade show meets in Las Vegas. This is the most important trade show that you attend. You also know that five trade publications cover your industry. You decide to sponsor the Annual Best Writing About Personal Financial Planning Award (my nomination goes to Andrew Tobias www.andrewtobias.com), and ask the sponsors if you can present the award at the annual banquet, which is part of many trade shows. Remind the sponsors that if they say yes, it's another way for their show to receive media coverage. Because this is your first year, you don't ask for submissions from the trade or consumer press. (Naturally, your company or organization issues a press release BEFORE the show indicating that you will present this award at the trade show. If you're really good, you'll get the trade organization to include the presentation of the award in all of its advertising literature.) You take all the issues of the five magazines that make the initial cut, which you've been glancing at throughout the year, and cull all those articles (that's 60 magazines if they're all monthlies) down to a choice of six to 10 articles. That should take about two to three hours. Then you hire two journalism professors to rate the articles. The magazine with the highest rating wins, and the one with the second most points finishes second. By removing yourself from the voting, you're above criticism. Indeed, you've demonstrated your fairness by asking for judges that are totally impartial. But what a way to swing for the fences and get publicity from these publications and a moment in the spotlight at the convention. Best of all, you can do it all over again next year.

Just like sponsoring a contest, a few basic rules apply. Choose an award that can be given annually, think of remaining above the fray when choosing a winner so that you can't be criticized, and bring the media into the picture as a participant, recipient or judge, whenever possible.

Tom's Tip: There should be a press release announcing the existence of the award, especially if you're seeking entries. Don't forget the press release AFTER you've given the award. A photo is mandatory.

I'm thinking of getting an award for the best book on publicity. The only problem is finding someone to sponsor it. Any takers?

Chapter 19

Social Service Organizations

Joining The Service For Publicity

The media is generally more open to writing about social service organizations and charities than a promotion or event that is strictly a business proposition. They usually feel that good deeds should receive a degree of coverage which they consider almost obligatory. By operating under this halo effect, you can obtain publicity for yourself and your company. This is often indirect publicity because it might be your participation or even leadership in a social service organization, like the Rotary, Kiwanis or Lions, on which the media focuses, but it's publicity nonetheless. The key questions are which organization to join and how to reap the benefits of publicity by drawing upon your connection to a social service organization.

In most cases, social service organizations have allied themselves with a particular cause. The Lions' commitment to helping people with vision problems is a perfect example. How can you argue with their fund-raising events and their goal to have people donate their used eyeglasses, which go to those who might not otherwise be able to afford them? It's a noble cause and a good one.

DISCLAIMER: Many of you reading this chapter will think: How mercenary! Joining an organization that benefits people only for the sake of using it to gain publicity.

That's NOT what I'm suggesting. I'm enough of a realist to know that with rare exceptions, few people will join an organization to accrue the publicity spillover from their membership. When you're looking to join a social service organization, it makes sense to find one that fits your own interests and notion of how you like to help people. If you hate to read aloud, I wouldn't suggest an organization that spends its time reading aloud to people with vision problems. Volunteering for an organization just for the sake of publicity probably won't work. If you don't enjoy the organization, you'll quit before you can reap the publicity reward. It's a poor way to spend your time (if publicity is one of your goals) because the real connection to an organization is when you can link yourself to its "automatic" press coverage. And this usually occurs when you've become an officer, which usually doesn't happen overnight or even in a few months. Most social service organizations now have Web sites or listings in the Yellow Pages that will tell you which branch of the organization is closest to you. Going on the Web will allow you to learn about the organization's history, goals and the nearest location to you in a matter of minutes.

But when you do become an officer of the organization or at least in charge of a committee, future news stories could easily mention your involvement. News stories about your organization will focus on the club's activities, but your name, occupation and even your business might find a mention in the story. This is especially true of a leadership position that could put you in the limelight both in the local press and also in the publication issued by the club or association that you joined.

Tom's Tips: Here are three tips that can give you publicity when joining a social service or charitable organization.

Tip One: Most social service organizations that are national have a publication about members, their branches and activities. Usually, they're very open to articles about your club and its activities. Indeed, they yearn for these types of articles. It's a great place to submit your article for publication. For example, you might consider writing about how your club conducted a successful fund drive by using an unusual marketing technique.

Tip Two: Another way to gain publicity is to mention to the person who's in charge of public relations for the organization that you've had a recent accomplishment and to ask if they could issue a press release based on that accomplishment. When I mentioned to my local Toastmasters' group that I had written *Wacky Days*, the vice president of public relations, immediately asked if she could issue a press release noting that "Local Toastmaster Writes A Book On Free Publicity." Smart move on her part because she thought of publicity for the club, and good move for me: added publicity for my book. The club is always looking for a way to be in the press. Positive news rubs both ways, promoting the club and highlighting the achievements of the individual.

Tip Three: If you join a social service organization and begin to look for a position, volunteer as soon as you can for the public relations job. Not because you'll suddenly "create" press releases that favor you, but because it will allow you entrée to the media. This is a great way to meet reporters and editors. I can assure you that they'll return your call much more quickly if you say you're calling on behalf of the Lions Club than if you're promoting your new thrift clothing store. Each time you send out a press release touting the accomplishments and activities of your club and members, you create an opportunity to meet members of the media and raise your visibility with editors and reporters. This is an immensely profitable use of your time as you begin to "know" several journalists to whom you're pitching press releases about the organization.

Tom Gets Idealistic: While we're on the topic of social service organizations and volunteerism, you should consider another reason for making even a modest commitment of time and effort. This is a book about publicity and not about working towards sainthood, but everyone should consider donating at least a small portion of their time to a social service organization that creates peace, harmony and a greater degree of tolerance in our communities. It is also fitting that you assist an organization that makes a tangible, positive effect in one's life, whether it's donating eyeglasses, reading a book to people who have poor eyesight or delivering a hot meal. If you think life is tough, I can assure you that compared to most people, your middle-class (or even lower-middle-class) existence is virtual opulence to most people in the world. Frankly, your problems really pale by comparison on the significant issues, when compared to people who suffer hardships every waking hour of their life: things like getting enough to eat, having a job and access to the necessary medicine to protect one's children. That's my do-gooder pitch, but I can assure you of one unassailable fact: If you pitch in at a social service or charitable organization, you'll not only be a candidate for possible publicity, you'll feel good about what you do and who you are. There aren't many things more important or rewarding than that, are there?

Chapter 20

Public Service Announcements

The Best Freebie You Can't Ignore

A Public Service Announcement (PSA) is an ideal way to obtain free coverage on radio or TV for your charity or not-for-profit organization. PSA's have a standard format you must follow (which I'll mention in a moment). What makes them valuable is the Federal Communications Commission once mandated that broadcast stations run PSA's as part of their obligation to dedicate a portion (small, of course) to the public good and to allow a certain degree of access to the public. According to a top broadcast lawyer, Cary Tepper, "Since 1980, the FCC no longer requires the broadcast of PSA's by radio and TV stations. However, PSA broadcasts help fulfill a station's general requirement to broadcast local, issues-oriented programming. So, most stations still broadcast a modest amount of PSA's."

There are five good reasons to use PSA's as a part of your publicity campaign. First, with the deregulation of the television industry in the 1980s, the horizon has changed for what PSA's stations will run. It used to be about health and safety, but now the range is much broader. As someone noted, public service has become public information. Second, with the spread of cable, commercial stations have more airtime, so the PSA is a viable option. Third, you can track your PSA through Nielsen's Sigma Electronic

Tracking to know when the station is airing it. Fourth, *PSA's are a great way to drive people to your organization's Web site* – even better if your business Web site sponsors the organization or provides a link. Fifth, you can often ask a celebrity, local, regional or even national, to appear in a PSA. You might be surprised how some will accommodate you. Try asking a well-known politician to deliver your PSA during election time and see what happens.

Many media outlets have the equivalent of a local or community calendar which they use to broadcast local happenings during newsbreaks or talk shows. Always check to see whether you can have the station broadcast your PSA during one of these shows. While I've heard of people giving their PSA information over the phone (or by e-mail), I would call the station to find out who is in charge, then ask for the person and ask if they prefer it by mail, fax or e-mail. A good idea is to send your media kit to the person responsible for PSA's and a second one to the news or program director (mentioning that you have submitted a PSA). The reason is that you will be giving extensive information about your group, implied via the PSA, that you are an active organization and that you would be happy to serve as a news source for any upcoming story that might fit your area of expertise. The station might accept a pre-recorded announcement or have someone in the studio "tape" the announcement. Be sure to ask.

Tom's Tip: Don't forget the most important rule for PSA's. Explain why the information you're asking them to air is important to the community.

Radio PSA. KISS (Keep It Simple Stupid)

I'm not calling you stupid, but it's important to keep in mind that you don't have a lot of time to deliver your message. So don't dilute it. Most radio PSA's will run 10, 20, 30, or 60 seconds. (A 60-second PSA is a real publicity hit.) Practice the PSA with a stopwatch. As a general rule, the word count versus time runs like this:

25 words = 10 seconds

50 words = 20 seconds
75 words = 30 seconds

Count digits (such as a phone number) as one word, and if you use long words, you will use up your time more quickly than the average I've provided. It's very important to keep your PSA focused on a single idea. The brevity of time simply doesn't allow for several ideas or mixed messages.

Don't forget to:

- ❑ Keep each announcement to one page.
- ❑ Double space the lines.
- ❑ Use line breaks at a natural point where the speaker would pause.
- ❑ Provide a cover letter with your PSA, especially if you're not providing a media kit.
- ❑ Provide a copy of the cover letter and the PSA to the person who handles the switchboard. This is important if listeners heard your PSA but didn't have time to get all the information. They might call asking for your phone number, a date, location, etc.
- ❑ **Important**. Don't include several messages in a PSA. Keep it to a single idea.

For a sample of a radio PSA, see the Appendix.

Television PSA. Television PSA's, while extremely effective, can present special problems. For a television PSA, you have to give the studio a professionally crafted tape, running from 10 to 60 seconds. Many stations no longer accept slides and written copy. It is also doubtful whether larger stations will accept three quarter or half-inch videotapes your VCR uses. Again, your best bet is to call the station and ask about their requirements. Be sure to ask for a written (or e-mail) copy if they provide it. Don't expect the station to pay for your video PSA. You will have to hire a professional videographer who can deliver the message with clarity and visual appeal. If you don't know of anyone, ask the studio for a recommendation. (They might recommend a staffer who moonlights.) When creating your tape, be sure to make it a second or two shorter than your time limit so that you (or the station) can add a "tag" which identifies the organization at the end of the PSA.

If you work for a nonprofit organization or are aligned with a worthy cause, PSA's provide an inexpensive, reliable and effective way to raise your visibility and your organization's while contributing to the betterment of society.

Chapter 21

Boards

When You Want To Be Board

I have participated in virtually every piece of advice or suggestion that appears in this book except for joining a board of a company or organization. (As I mentioned, I've been quite successful at placing clients on editorial boards.) So my information is secondhand, but I've always thought that joining a board is a reasonable, reliable approach to gaining publicity. There are business-type boards where either you entreat experienced business people to sit on your board, and they offer their advice for running your company, or you serve the same function for someone else's company. You can obtain a small amount of publicity in this by issuing press releases about your joining the board (with a photo, please!) and subsequent joint press releases. Issuing press releases based on your membership of a business board has some publicity potential, but the real benefit usually comes from joining the board of a not-for-profit or charitable organization that is more prone to getting free publicity.

Being on a board works in much the same way that joining a social service organization does (see Chapter 19). That means you must be active, you must involve yourself in the aspects of the organization that gain the most publicity, and you must work to be on the end of the organization, if possible, which deals with the media. Boards tied to a public service or charitable organization often have drawing power that a business usually lacks. As a board member, especially if you're really more than window dressing, you have the aura of the board as another outlet for publicity. For example, as mentioned, your entry to the board is news. You might want to write an Op-Ed piece (remember Chapter 12) about some event or position the board has taken. In a sense, you've just gained another outlet of expression and a new perspective or expertise with which to contact the media. If you live in a city large enough, your newspaper probably carries a list of new board appointees.

Just being on the board tacitly implies that you're an expert about whatever issues the board raises in conjunction with its mission and activities.

Tom's Tip: Most people serve on a board for one or two years. This means you can't just join whenever you want. Here's what you should do:

1) Make a list of five boards that you would feel comfortable joining and to which you could contribute. If one or more gets regular media coverage in your area, so much the better.
2) Call the organization and ask what qualifications they look for when choosing individuals to join their board. Be sure they send you relevant information such as an application, mission statement, etc. Ask how much "lead" time is necessary for them to consider you as a candidate for the board and to whom should you send your application. Be sure that you mark your calendar and contact the organization at the right time. This could mean you might have to wait a few weeks to even a year. That's an advantage. The few people who are savvy enough to think of this approach won't follow through in nine months. It's human nature. (I place a reminder in my computer's "tickler" system. Nine months later – be sure you backup your calendar – the reminder "drops" down on me.)

3) By trying five organizations, you will probably reduce the "wait" for an opening slot. Again, if you land one, don't follow up on the others unless you intend to make a legitimate contribution.

Joining a board isn't a quick way to gain publicity. It is a goal you can attain, and this approach offers the fragrance of adding your name to the cachet value of the organization that can be quite powerful. It's worth considering. The icing is that some boards actually pay their members for participating. Just like joining a social service organization, the more you have in common with the organization and its goals, the more likely you'll be an asset to them while you reap some free publicity.

A few thoughts about boards (and the advice they offer).

In those days he was wiser than he is now; he used frequently to take my advice.
Winston Churchill, statesman, winner of the Nobel Prize for literature

The only thing to do with good advice is to pass it on; it is never of any use to oneself.
Oscar Wilde, author

Chapter 22

Directory Of Experts

Look It Up, I'm The Expert

As I've repeated throughout this book, much of the publicity that you gain from the media comes from their belief that you're some type of expert or authority, even if this belief is implicit. Finding your name in directories or lists to which your potential customer or client base refers is an excellent way to gain credibility and publicity. Even if your entry in a directory doesn't give you new business, it adds to the halo effect that you are an authority in your field. The advantage to appearing in directories is that after the initial outlay in terms of effort and time, you're almost permanently a member of that directory as long as you respond to their annual (or even more infrequent) requests for updated information.

With a few exceptions, I'm talking about directories that DO NOT require you to pay. My mantra is that if it's free, it's for me. (My other mantra is that if it's free, take three.) I (mostly) hate spending money on directories.

Which directories should list you? It's a basic question, and you answer it by asking yourself another basic question: What directories would my potential customers or clients look at if they were seeking my type of product or service? I would develop as extensive a list as I could think of and divide it into two categories, free and those for which you must pay. I would write to each directory that offers a free listing and obtain an entry. The directories that require payment are something I would examine *very* carefully.

Let's deal first with directories that require payment. I'm in the publicity or PR business, and the bible is *O'Dwyer's* directory, which lists your big-time PR firms. I can't possibly imagine that appearing in *O'Dwyers* will bring me any business. During my first two years in business, I had a listing in the Yellow Pages under Public Relations Agencies. Since I was a one-man shop, I know what calls came in. I never, not once, received a phone call from *anyone* inquiring about my services, despite a reasonably impressive client list. During that time, they included one of the largest business-to-business publishers in the country, the 25th largest privately owned company in the United States and one of the largest architectural firms in my home state. (I did receive a few phone inquiries once I switched to the speaking bureaus section because of my public speaking engagements. But not one referral or query based on my publicity business.) My practice has strictly been a referral business, and when the size of my clients finally grew large enough, I was able to take mom-and-pop referrals (and I don't mean this in a pejorative way) and refer them to other public relations people who were more suited to serving them. Directories just never applied to my business. Why would I pay to be in a directory when I simply never got clients that way?

But some savvy business people figured out that the best market for selling directories are the people who have a listing IN the directories. In other words, the listing is free, but you have to buy the directory if you want to own one. Obviously, they're appealing to the ego of the person who submits an entry. Some people, whether or not they buy a directory, do so because it allows them to include the entry as a component of their resume. This might make sense for people starting out in a career. However, I don't believe they're particularly effective once your career has taken off.

Tom's Tip: If a directory is free, go ahead and take advantage of a listing. You might actually get a lead or prospect, and you can include your entry, if you choose to, in your promotion bio. (Don't forget to keep the information updated.) So are there directories that make sense? Absolutely! If you're a magazine and have a listing in *Writer's Market,* which in essence is a directory of publications, it makes complete sense. Magazines, for example, especially those that are brand new, can obtain an entry and immediately gain credibility and forge an identity by appearing in this bible that freelance writers refer to all the time. Editors also use it to attract their clients or customers (that means writers), who contribute articles to the publication. Finally, they can nip in the bud many requests from writers who want to know about their editorial likes and dislikes. They know that most professional writers will first look in the book (or online) before bothering an editor with a query.

As a general rule, DON'T pay for entries in most directories if you must pay, nor should you bother buying the directory.

There are three types of directories or online services that you **MIGHT** want to consider. You have to pay to play with these three. I'm not making a judgment either way, but I can say that I've used all three and was pleased. The question for you is whether the number of inquiries from the press will be worth the expense.

As a journalist, I often used *The Yearbook of Experts*©. The problem is that I don't know how extensively anyone else uses this book or how it has changed since the Internet has come into vogue. It was the easiest way to find national experts. I remember once when I worked as the business editor on a daily newspaper, the city editor left the staff instructions we were to follow while he was on vacation. He left a note saying I should be the one to write a particular story because I was adept at finding national experts. Well, that was fairly easy. I simply turned to my

Yearbook. Now, in the Internet age, this directory also has a Web site, www.yearbook.com. Those who buy space in the directory also get a listing on their Web site and a link. They built this business by sending their directories to media personnel throughout the country. A member of the media only has to request a free copy of the directory on their letterhead. I recently e-mailed my request, and they quickly sent me a copy. I am the editor of two national magazines, so the request was legitimate from a journalism standpoint, rather than from my position running a public relations consulting firm.

PRNewswire is a company that offers electronic press releases to the media, and it also offers a service called *Profnet*. Originally it was an organization mostly comprised of academics, who were experts in various areas. A reporter would simply call up, explain that he was writing a story about antique cars, and they would give him any names of experts they had in their database on antique cars. PRNewswire bought the service and now offers it electronically to journalists.

They promise to promptly send a query from a journalist to information officers in the next of three daily transmissions to their 11,000 members. This service is **ONLY** open to legitimate public relations firms and public information officers (like me). It costs thousands, but it's a good service.

For more information about this service, go to www.prnewswire.com.

BusinessWire is a company similar to PRNewswire. It has a similar service which they call *ExpertSource*. They provide far fewer requests for information from journalists, but the service is very inexpensive. For more information, go to www.businesswire.com.

Chapter 23

Conventions

Meeting Your Publicity Needs Face To Face

Nearly every business person who is serious about the industry in which they operate belongs to an organization that fosters and promotes its fellow members and the industry. Also, your customers, especially in the business-to-business world, have organizations which they join. This means that your customers and potential customers have conventions which they attend because they hope to make contacts that will lead to sales. Business people also attend conventions to learn how to conduct their business more effectively and efficiently, gain trade information and sometimes just to socialize. (Think of it as continuing education opportunities.) You should join an organization within your own industry and become active in it so that you raise your visibility. You can accomplish this by volunteering, at least initially, for a committee position. You'll find that most committees welcome volunteers. Be sure to fulfill your promises and commitments and demonstrate your enthusiasm, friendliness and industry savviness. If this route is particularly pleasing to you – the meetings, camaraderie and tasks are interesting and fun – strive to move up in the organization. Your membership and, more importantly, your leadership role raise your credibility and give you publicity opportunities via the organization which you might not have as an individual.

If you're in the business-to-business world, attending conventions that your potential clients or customers attend is a target to which you should aim. It's a great place to find new clients and brighten the halo around your expertise (I'll explain this shortly), and it'll allow you the opportunity to socialize with current clients. Always remember what good publicity does: It brings you new business but it also creates that golden glow around you, which reassures your *existing* clients or customers that they've made the right choice. It's amazing how hard we try to obtain new customers and how frequently we begin to forget about them once we've landed the account. The old adage is absolutely true: Your best customer is the one you have already.

But going to a convention that your potential clients or customers attend for new business is not enough. What you really want to do is go to the conference or convention as an expert presenter. Here's how you do it. Make a list of all the conventions that you feel are important for obtaining new clients or reassuring current clients. Find out when they have an annual convention (in some cases, organizations have two meetings a year, one is the annual conference and the second is a smaller business meeting). Try to track down the convention information from the previous year and see if you can find out information about the current year. Track down the person who is responsible for choosing speakers or presenters. This person often operates under the rubric of director of education, or if the organization is large enough, they might have one person dedicated entirely to the task of the convention. Call that person and say you would like to be a presenter at the next conference. Ask them what type of information they look for when they choose presenters. Let the person tell you how you should "sell" your expertise to them. Someone might say, "send us a couple of potential topics," while someone else might focus on your public speaking background. Another person might require a videocassette of you speaking. After they've revealed the best way to pitch them, do exactly what they say and include your media and expertise kit. (I'm sure this will be part of their request.) If you can determine 10 different conventions that you could attend as a speaker or presenter and even obtain one engagement your first year, you're moving in the right direction. Create a media kit that clearly demonstrates your expertise and highlights any previous speaking engagements. (See the Appendix that gives an example of what a media kit should contain.) This reassures people that you're worth listening to because you're an expert and that you probably won't suffer from a tangled tongue when speaking to this group. Send it to the person who makes decisions about speakers NINE months before the convention date and follow-up with a phone call. Better yet, when you talk with the person in charge of booking speakers, ask them when you should submit your information in a timely fashion. Send it too soon and your info will disappear in a pile from which no one will ever retrieve it. Send it too late and you'll have to wait a year to try again.

Tom's Tip: Here's a way to create a positive image, land a speaking engagement and raise your visibility.

First, if the person responsible for booking speakers indicates that they've filled all the speaking slots, offer to fillin if someone cancels out. That means leaving a slot open in your calendar even though you're not committed to anything. S--- happens. I was at a convention in Baltimore, and one of the speakers couldn't fly in because of a hurricane in Florida. The organizers had to find a fillin at the last minute.

Second, about two weeks BEFORE the convention, send a note or a postcard again stating that you would be happy to help and fillin if someone cancels. Even if your contact person doesn't call, be assured that they will remember you the next time they think about booking speakers for the next convention. They will remember you and be far more approachable when you return to them with the idea of speaking to their group.

Third, and most important: Don't be discouraged. If you view publicity as a long-term effort, it might take several years to break down the doors of a convention where you would really like to speak. (Yes, a few years. That's why they call it persistence.) Unless you're retiring in the next few years, chasing after the person who makes those decisions for a slot on their speaking agenda often pays major dividends. It's all a matter of how important you feel the organization or convention attendees might be for future business. By speaking at the convention, you'll have the confirmation of the sponsoring organization that: 1) You're an expert (why else would you be a presenter?); 2) You have something worthwhile to say (why else would they give you a platform?). Be sure, and I can't stress this enough, that every handout you have at the convention (and you MUST leave a leave-behind or handout) contains ways to contact you.

Several other aspects of speaking at conventions make it perfect for publicizing your name. The most important is that by virtue of being a speaker, you're often included in the preconvention publicity and advertising at no cost. It's great for you and your company to receive this free publicity. Second, clearly you will have the opportunity to express yourself as an expert, and this will hopefully result in your obtaining more customers and clients – certainly leads – after your speech. Third, in some instances, you might actually be able to sell your product. (I would generally caution against this, however.) Convention planners expect speakers to be objective and fair. The lectern isn't a place for a nonstop sales pitch. (But you might allow yourself one or two minutes to "sell." You must check out the rules regarding this with the association's convention director.)

Finally, it's far easier to receive a return engagement or a crossover into another convention sponsored by the organization once you've already spoken and they've had a chance to witness your performance and their members' reaction to it. If you do a good job, convention directors will remember you for future assignments. Most convention directors talk to each other in and within related industries. This is a great way to have someone promote you if you have given them a satisfactory or great presentation. Indeed, you should make it a policy to ask for a referral letter if you can get one. Be prepared to write it yourself. Then use a copy of that letter when you call upon similar organizations. It marks you as someone familiar with their industry and not just a generalist.

Tom's Tip: Medium-to-large cities generally sponsor conventions and meetings ranging from local to national in nature. The starting point should be your local and regional Convention and Visitors Bureau (CVB). They probably publish a weekly or monthly list of upcoming conventions and meetings. In all likelihood, they know who's coming a year in advance. Ask for the list and don't hesitate to explain why you want one. Sometimes you might have to join the CVB to obtain an advance copy, but the fee for a small business can be quite modest. If you have the time, meet with the person at the CVB who handles these meetings and explain what you do, why certain groups might want to hear your message and how you're willing to speak on short notice. Then target these groups that will be visiting your area. Find out who is responsible for the convention and contact that person, offering your services as a speaker or presenter. Stress the fact that you're local. The proximity of your location will appeal to people from the organization sponsoring the convention who might need a speaker on short notice because they know you'll be able to reach their convention with no travel considerations and they won't have to pay the usual travel expenses. Remember my Florida hurricane example. It also helps to stay in touch with the local CVB and explain your willingness to stand in on short notice. Often the organization having the convention will turn to the CVB contact for a fill-in speaker. Again, use common sense. If you only talk about cat breeding, you probably have an uphill climb. I speak about getting free publicity, and virtually every business or not-for-profit is interested in my subject, so I have broad appeal.

If you are reasonably good at giving speeches or presentations, working the convention crowd can be immensely helpful in making contacts. I read a confidential report today about two national trade organizations that are considering a merger. In this confidential report, they asked members of both organizations what was the greatest benefit they derived from attending their annual conventions. The answer was clear and direct: networking. Do you know how many times I see people remain after a speech to talk with the speaker? Do you know how many times I see an exchange of business cards? It's called a hot lead. When you get that AND the publicity, I consider it a home run with someone on base.

Tom's Tip: When you've attended the convention, write a testimonial to the person in charge. Let them know that you would be happy to allow your testimonial to be used for the publicity campaign the organization conducts to boost their convention attendance. I've done it, and believe me: It works. Free publicity to a core audience you wish to influence, and you don't pay. A wonderful tactic.

Chapter 24

Radio

Sunday, Sunday, At Tommy's Drag Raceway

Do you recall those radio advertisements with the booming voice that said, "SUNDAY, SUNDAY, AT _________ (fill in the blank) DRAG RACEWAY. For those of you old enough to remember, they were loud, obnoxious commercials drumming up business for drag racing. If you listened to the radio, you couldn't get away from the ads. They were everywhere. Radio is alive and well (and it didn't die because of television, though that was the prediction). I tend to like radio journalists because they remind me of print journalists with more outward fire. Because their sword and armor is the spoken word, they talk a lot, too, which is an occupational hazard.

I've had excellent success landing my clients on radio stations throughout the United States. In some ways, getting interviews via the radio is quite easy. If you don't know what you're doing, it can be a waste of time. Here's why.

The principle for appearing on a radio station in New York City is the same as Boise, Idaho. The difference, of course, is that the competition to "appear" on radio in New York City is difficult. Much more difficult. Simple fact: The larger the listening audience based on demographic rankings, the more you're competing with other potential guests, like yourself, who think radio is a good vehicle for getting a message out. Publicity over the radio, when it's free, is a great tool.

Jack Canfield and Mark Victor Hansen, the authors of *Chicken Soup For the Soul*, have sold more than 60 MILLION books and swear by radio's effectiveness for publicity and promoting products.

Radio can be an **especially** effective and profitable publicity approach if you have a product or service that has **mass consumer appeal**. It's a particularly effective way to sell books. I know of one author who self-publishes his books (earning about 80 to 90 percent of the gross revenue) and says he won't go to a mainstream publisher because he can't afford to. He sells the majority of his books via radio appearances.

You have to make an important decision before you pursue radio as a tool for publicity. Do you want national exposure or are you only interested in local publicity? In short, does your real audience encompass a local, regional or national target? The rules for getting airtime for free publicity are virtually the same. The only difference is the size of the net that you cast as you attempt to become a radio presence.

Just remember that if your topic has universal appeal, virtually all radio stations throughout the country will be interested.

Here's why radio is such a great way to obtain free publicity and what you have to do to obtain it.

1. **What Makes Radio Such A Great Publicity Machine?** Radio is extremely effective as a publicity tool because you can use it regardless of where you live. Most radio station interviews occur over the phone. At times, your interview might be "live," which means it is being broadcast as you speak, or the interview is simply taped for later use. Either way, it's incredibly easy to do. You can be in your pajamas, at your desk sipping coffee and reading the newspaper, or just daydreaming. (Until you get more comfortable with someone asking you questions, however,

you might want to ensure that you've "prepped" yourself for the interview. That means you have notes in front of you in case you hit the mental wall and forget what you want to say.) Also, because so many people listen to radio while in their cars, you have, to some degree, a captive audience. They might switch to another station, but they won't go to sleep on you.

2. **Who Should You Contact at a Radio Station?** Your best bet to appear on radio is to approach a producer or news director of a radio station that has a "talk" format. This doesn't mean the news department of a radio station with a music format can't or won't interview you, but talk shows are your best possibilities because they are always on the lookout for guests. It is critical to remember that the radio landscape, like daily journalism and television, changes constantly. (This is somewhat less true of the trade press, though this segment of the media also has a high turnover rate.) You can pitch your idea to the host of a radio show. Indeed, some hosts also serve as the "producer". It is the job of the radio producer or news director to find guests for their shows. When in doubt, send your information to the producer.

3. **How Do You Find Out Which Radio Stations Might Be Interested In Your Topic?** It's easy. If your interest is strictly local, just check the local Yellow Pages or several directories that would include the adjoining counties and copy down the addresses and telephone numbers. Address your mailing to the producer, unless you have the name of the host for a specific show that interests you. For example, if you own a restaurant in Santa Fe, it might be ego-warming to talk about a mix of Northern Italian-Mexican cuisine to a Seattle station, but it probably won't bring you any additional business. Appearing on local radio is your target. That might mean going outward of 100 miles (you'd better have a great restaurant for someone to drive 100 miles one way). All the stations in that area would comprise your radio media list. If you're the author of

a book, in addition to owning a restaurant, it makes sense to appeal to radio stations everywhere. It also makes sense to focus on other geographic regions if you have a specific reason. Using our example, if you're planning to open a similar restaurant in Seattle, you should consider targeting the Seattle area.

Another easy way to obtain a list of local media is to buy a local media guide if one exists in your city. Most larger American cities have a press club which often publishes these guides. Sometimes, such as in Cleveland, the not-for-profit Federation for Community Planning publishes the local media guide. (And a terrific guide it is.) A local guide will serve your local or regional needs.

If you want to appear on radio throughout the country, you must purchase a media list. There are several ways to accomplish this. You can buy or rent mailing labels for radio stations from various media sources such as *Bacon's* (see Chapter 5 This is fine if you are positive that you will only target radio stations once or twice a year. My database for radio (see my earlier comments about media databases in Chapter 5) lists 4,600 radio stations throughout the United States ranging from the No. 1 market based on potential listening audience (Greater New York City) to the smallest (North Platte, Nebraska, No. 208). Now, of those radio stations, 964 have some type of talk format. Those 964 radio stations are my target audience for my clients. Yes, there are some special programs, with a theme such as business, which I'll mention shortly, and yes, my database misses a few, but my list has a solid sampling of stations with talk shows. The nice thing about radio (and television) stations is that they don't disappear with the frequency that print publications, especially magazines, do.

4. **What Do Radio Station Producers And News Directors Look For When Booking Guests?** It's a familiar refrain that you've read earlier and one on which I will continue to harp: If you can provide the radio show

with information that is relevant, useful or interesting to the listeners' lives or businesses, you have a greater chance of appearing as a guest. *Failing this criteria, you must entertain the listeners.* If you're in the business-to-business world, your task of appearing on radio is far more difficult, and you have to change your approach.

Consumer Products or Service: Let's start with consumer issues. If your product or service has mass appeal and a consumer-oriented focus, you have a great shot at getting a reasonable number of appearances, or "hits," as I like to refer to them. This is particularly true if you've written a book. (Producers who book radio guests love authors – remember that chapter on writing a book?) Here's what I mean. You have an outstanding chance of getting on radio if you can pitch the idea that you're the expert on: 12 Ways To Lose 12 Pounds 12 Weeks Before Summer (Diet or Nutrition Expert); Unknown Beauty Secrets With Common Household Items (Beauty Expert); Saving $5,000 Per Year Regardless Of Your Income (Personal Finance Expert); or How To Track Down Your Ancestors (Genealogy Expert).

Business Products or Service: If you're in the software business and you've created a software program that helps improve the logistics process at manufacturing and distribution facilities, any radio program that focuses on business is fair game. Indeed, this should be the first group that you try to approach as a potential guest. You might discuss how virtually any business, once it improves its logistics, can save at least 20 percent in costs during the next year, even if it's a small firm with only five employees. You might want to discuss how a businessperson decides to venture into a new area – in this case, the manufacturing and distribution sector – and what elements must be conquered before you give the green light. The process, in this instance, might interest business listeners even if they have nothing to do with software. Every businessperson with one employee or 10,000 thinks about venturing into a new territory. They would probably appreciate the general principles that you could offer.

But how do you offer this same information to a consumer-based audience which makes up the vast majority of listeners on radio stations? It can be difficult. In the example I gave, you might send the radio station a fact sheet that says 42 percent of their listening audience is engaged in either manufacturing or distribution, and they can enhance their careers by sharing tips with the boss that will have an immediate impact on the bottom line. You then proceed to outline how these people can go back to work the next day with a few workable suggestions and impress the boss with their initiative. That's the angle you pitch.

A True Story: I represent Arthur St. Onge, an international expert on mass customization and logistics strategies and the president of York, Pa.-based The St. Onge Co., (www.stonge.com). Appearing on consumer-oriented radio shows provided a vexing problem because generally Art has a business perspective in his role as an adviser to several dozen Fortune 1,000 companies. I had the problem of connecting the strategic business approach of mass customization to the listening consumer. It wasn't easy. I understood that the ultimate function (or end user) of mass customization is the consumer, the very people who listen to most talk shows. Taking that view, I managed to have Art "appear" on radio stations throughout the United States explaining mass customization, which industries are involved, who will join the trend and, most importantly, **what it means to the consumer**. (You can now "customize" your jeans, perfume, bicycle and cereal. Each year, more items that you mass ordered in the past will be "customized" just for you.) It also helps when you have a guest such as Art, who is articulate, engaging, enthusiastic and knows his topic cold.

In Art's case, a few stations even invited him back for a *second* interview within a few months because they were so pleased with his appearance. Art has an excellent speaking presence. I suspect he honed his skills as a featured speaker at industry meetings and conventions for more than a decade.

This is a good time to mention that if you are concerned about your speaking mannerisms, if you "freeze" at the thought of being on the radio or if you speak with an accent that makes you difficult to understand for most English speakers, it might be wise to have another member of your staff serve as the interviewee. (Or join Toastmasters to develop skills that will improve your performance.)

5. **What Do You Say On A Radio Show?** Address the issue for which you suggested the radio show interview. If you have a product to pitch, that's great (why else would you want to be on the show?), but you can't be a nonstop commercial plugging your book, product or service. You MUST share information that is instructive, helpful and entertaining. Don't cheat the listeners. Focus on the more common thread, which is what you know and how it will affect the listeners of the show. Timeliness also helps. I know of an author who wrote a book on preparing recipes during Passover. Guess when she begins her campaign to appear on radio? Correct. About a month before Passover. The more you can add a timely twist to your topic, the greater your chance of provoking interest from a radio producer.

OK, so now that you have an idea that you believe is timely, interesting and saleable, and you're an expert because you want to hawk a book you've written, what next?

You copy my creation: The Guest Alert. (See Appendix for an example.) I'd never heard of this until I invented it. So I take all the credit. You simply adapt the Media Alert, which I've discussed earlier, to a radio format. Be sure to be blunt. Write, "Why This Topic Will Grab Your Listeners' Attention". Then in simple, clear and dramatic fashion, explain why the producer should book you. And you'd better be able to support it. Let me take a shot. Using the example of household items that can improve your appearance, you have a book and want to promote it. You answer the basic facts in the Guest Alert and then you ask: "Why will this topic grab your reader's attention?" You answer it with: "Every woman in America spends an average of $231.22 on cosmetics each year to create a new look or to enhance their current look. Every man in America spends $177.22 an average on cosmetics for the same reasons. For less than $33 per year, you can dramatically reduce your cosmetic bill; you can use national, everyday items available in your house to look more attractive. Immediately."

Whew, there it is. (My imagination created the figures.) Now what producer, radio talk show host or news director wouldn't want you to be on their show? But you had better be able to back this up. You MUST deliver on what you promise.

When you send these Guest Alerts, some additional material should accompany them. Be sure to include:

1. A list of potential questions the radio host could (or should) ask. This is a great time to write a few softball questions for yourself, especially at the beginning. However, don't totally avoid controversy, especially if that's what you're promoting. Send at least five questions but not more than 10. (As a general rule, I always send 10.) The talk show host will need a warm-up, and he also doesn't want to appear dumb. Your questions will serve as a great starting point. (If you're a PR person, be sure to run those questions by your client who is the potential guest.) This helps protect the guest from being blindsided.) Art St. Onge went through the questions with me before he began his radio career.

Tom's Tip: If you begin to appear on enough radio shows, this will happen sooner or later – the host will sandbag you. What that means is that regardless of your good intentions, you'll have a host who will mock, ridicule or insult you. It might be nothing more than the host got up grouchy that morning. My advice: **Forget about it**. It doesn't happen with most shows (unless you actually seek that type of format). Immediately try to book yourself on the next possible show.

2. Include a "fact sheet" that makes your topic interesting. Elaborate in one or two pages on the highlights that you're going to discuss. Highlight, in bullet format, the main points about which you'll be talking. Keep the fact sheet to one or two pages.

3. Include one to three pages of background to elaborate on the proposed subject you're offering. For example, a two-page news story of how the average American simply can't get enough of beauty tips would bolster your case. I like to include a news story as background because it lends a sense of importance to your idea. If the media is writing about it, won't listeners be interested?

A quick word about authorship and appearing as a guest on radio. You'll notice that I use many author examples. It is truly the shortcut to radio appearances. What if you don't have a book? You must then use your job, experience, education and industry position to promote your expertise. Using the previous example, if you don't have a book but own a cosmetic store, the way to promote your expertise might be: "Angel Jones has been the owner of Natural Cosmetics for more than 10 years and is an industry leader in promoting low-cost, natural solutions to beauty". See, you're not an author, you ARE an expert.

Welcome To The Graduate School Of Radio Publicity.

While I've had excellent success placing clients on radio stations, there is another approach that might be more difficult and certainly takes more effort. However, this approach, pioneered by radio guest guru Alex Carroll, is also worth pursuing, especially if you have a product or service that you wish to sell to the public throughout the United States.

At last count, Alex Carroll has appeared on more than 1,112 radio shows pitching his book, *Beat The Cops, The Guide To Fighting Your Traffic Ticket And Winning,* which describes how to beat speeding tickets. He's been on radio so often that he wrote an excellent book about how to appear as a guest on radio shows. I bought the book myself (after making my own successful foray into radio) and recommend it highly. There are two aspects to Alex's approach that are significantly different from the way I conduct my campaign. I've been so impressed that I'm going to modify my own approach because of the impact that his technique offers. Here's the Alex Carroll approach.

First, Alex calls the producer and, with a written script in front of him, he offers to be a guest on the show. Now this is important. Alex admits that it can take an average of 10 calls before he actually gets a booking. Sometimes, he points out, he gets the producer on the phone and he immediately schedules Alex as a guest. Keep in mind that Alex's product or topic is broad. (His book explains how to fight traffic tickets in court, which means if you're a driver, you're a candidate for his book. Who hasn't gotten at least one traffic ticket?)

Alex has developed the art of how to pitch your product (in Alex's case, his book) on the radio. Alex's book, *The Radio Publicity Manual*, describes it in great detail.

The other approach Alex uses is that he's created his own radio database. This is important. While I've used the database supplied by Radio TV Interview Report (RTIR) (as has Alex), his complaint was that while he appeared on more than 40 stations, only three produced phone calls that resulted in any significant sales of his book. Taking the initiative, he developed a database which lists only the producers and contact points with the radio stations that have the largest listening audiences in the United States. He now sells this database. I have it, and it's excellent. Because it's in an electronic format and updated annually, it's current, which is important because of the high turnover in journalism, particularly in the broadcast field.

If your goal is to appear on radio stations, then a mass mailing, which I conduct successfully, is a good approach. It works for me because I have faith in my ability to pique the interest of radio producers. My media alerts are successful because I know what producers look for.

If you're going to use radio in any fashion, Alex's book, at the very least, is absolutely worth the investment. If you want to really hit the big time, as Alex has done, **and you want to sell a product or service**, his database will help you get there. (Contact Alex for his book or database at www.radiopublicity.com and tell him that Tom sent you.)

A key point: No matter what topic you're pitching in terms of publicity, it must have wide appeal. The only exception is a radio show that focuses on a subject which matches your topic. (You pitched a gardening topic to a garden talk show.)

Look at Alex's book. If you drive a car in the United States, you're a potential buyer of Alex's book on fighting traffic tickets. Most people who drive have had a police officer stop them at some point in their driving life, and everyone I know has received at least one speeding ticket in their life.

Here's another example. If you find a legal way to increase your benefits from social security, you have information that would presumably have an impact on every American that works. In both of these cases, the net is very wide, and that's what radio hosts look for.

But if you've just designed a new bow that will increase accuracy for archery enthusiasts, you've got a problem. No matter how significant the discovery is, the only people who care are other archers and those in the bow hunting business.

Which begs the question: "OK, Tom, you're such a hotshot, how would you pitch the archery breakthrough?"

First, I would find every outdoors-related show (and publication) and pitch it as a straight archery story.

Second, I would find every business-related show and pitch it as a business story. (Yes, Ralph, if you're selling it, then it becomes a business story.)

Third, and here's where I earn my fee, I'd pitch it as a human-interest story. I'd show that there hasn't been a technological breakthrough in archery for more than 200 years. I'd show how all my friends thought I was crazy for giving up most of my activities and burying myself in my basement for two years as I toiled away trying to achieve "The Perfect Bow." The title of my pitch: "How An Ex-Postman Designed The Most Efficient And Accurate Killing Bow In History." Finally, I'd point out that 20 percent of the world champions used my bow within three years of its introduction.

Staple my mantra on your eyelids: It's about people and ideas.

You can also try to use gimmicks to get on a radio show. This usually works for getting on local stations and can be effective when done properly. (See the gimmicks explanation in the next chapter on television.)

Final Word On Radio. Alex Carroll's detailed and creative approach to using radio for publicity is impressive. Because of his expertise, I asked him what were the three most common reasons that people *did not* succeed at using radio for an effective publicity campaign, especially if they were selling a product or service.

Here's what he wrote, exclusively for the readers of *Wacky Days*:

Failure Reason No. 1: They target little stations instead of big ones (usually unknowingly), and they fail to ask for the drive-time slots ... where the listenership is at its highest. This isn't rocket science ... the more people who hear you, the bigger your response will be.

Failure Reason No. 2: They try to sell the producer on the merits of their book or product, instead of the show they are going to put on for his audience. Producers really don't care about what you're selling. They only care about whatever you are going to tell their audience – will it entertain or enlighten them?

Failure Reason No. 3: They are not persistent. They make one phone call to a producer, leave a message on his voice mail, and when they don't hear back from him, they give up. They fail to understand how busy producers are ... and that unless they are a celebrity, producers will not normally call them back. They must keep calling until they actually get the producer on the phone.

If you have a product or service that appeals to a broad group of people, you have priced it "right" for the retail market, and you enjoy talking about it in an interesting and inspiring way, take it to the airwaves and prepare for the cash register to ring. If you don't believe me, ask Alex Carroll.

A few thoughts about radio.

Radio wasn't outside our lives. It coincided with – and helped to shape – our childhood and adolescence. As we slogged toward maturity, it also grew up and turned into television, leaving behind, like dead skin, transistorized talk-radio and nonstop music shows.
Vincent Canby, writer

BBC Radio is a never-never land of broadcasting, a safe haven from commercial considerations, a honey pot for every scholar and every hare-brained nut to stick a finger into.
Morley Safer, journalist

Chapter 25

Television

"It's A Bird...It's A Plane... It's YOU...

There is probably no medium that will make you a "name" or a celebrity as quickly or as forcefully as television. It pervades every facet of our communications-dependent society and correspondingly has a stunning impact, able to immediately transmit ideas, stories and visual images that are overwhelming. Television is a tough nut to crack on any regular basis. Selling stories to television is difficult, and selling a story idea for national coverage is even more challenging. You can do it, but the competition is ferocious.

Television makes for an interesting comparison with its broadcast counterpart, radio. Television is more powerful because of its visual impact. It wears a straitjacket, however, when it comes to the issue of the scope of coverage. Most stories are local or have a slightly regional focus, while the major networks and a few other television news organizations cover the "national" stories. There's really nothing in between. It's rare that a local television station will run 500 miles to cover a story in another city unless there's a connection to the hometown.

Radio, on the other hand, as I've mentioned previously, is a favorite of mine because stations will interview you regardless of where you live. The entire country is a potential target for publicity. All you need is a telephone. In short, geography usually doesn't matter.

But television requires you to think about whether you pitch your ideas as strictly a local story or one with a national slant. (It's true that many local stories become part of the focus by the national media, but this is because the local station "feeds" the story to its network headquarters.) You have no control over this other than suggesting it. Believe me, if the local television person has any news instinct and sees the possibility for national pickup, they'll forward the story. A good example is bad weather. There's a story about a blizzard, and all of a sudden Peter Jennings shows a snowstorm in Cleveland. While the storm is, obviously, a story in Cleveland, the footage for the national story is borrowed from the ABC affiliate in Cleveland.

A few general rules about television. If you think that time is precious in radio, wait until you take a crack at television. Try this. Watch the evening news and discount the stories that you can't compete against, which include crime, disasters, political shenanigans, etc. That leaves literally a few stories as features. Those usually have a visual impact often tied to an event.

If you're trying for a news segment, you must really have an eye-catching, audience-appealing idea that's not only dramatic but visual. It's amazing how many people forget this obvious fact. Television journalists think not only about "the story" but also about "what's the visual." Put simply, you must have a very strong hook or angle to attract a camera crew to your place of business or organization. Event-driven publicity might be the easiest, especially if there is a not-for-profit or charity component to your event. When contacting a television station, besides the usual press release or media alert, I would create a visual alert. In short, I'd actually make some suggestions that would explain to the producer, news editor or assignment editor what the camera crew can expect. Here's where you must tell the editor exactly what visuals you can offer. For example, if you suggest a story to an editor that no one else can duplicate because you're offering the only Siberian tigers within a radius of 500 miles and they've just given birth, you'll probably get a camera crew. If you also have or can obtain official sanction, you'll have a better chance. Official sanction or partnering means the person or event has some official status within the media market. (City government, well-known not-for-profits, colleges, or charitable organizations are examples.) They usually obtain some degree of "automatic" coverage based upon their official function. A mayor's office is another good example of this. In most towns, if a mayor has a press conference, the media will respond. If the mayor wants to have a one-on-one session with a reporter, the media outlet will send someone. I was responsible for obtaining coverage during National Tourism Week for a large American city. All four major television stations sent reporters, the major daily newspaper showed up (big photo the next day, too), and we had interviews with a few radio stations. What made this work, in addition to the careful timing of a press release, a media alert, calling each television station and having an attention-getting gimmick with the releases, was the official linkage to the city (after all, it was the "mayor" and it was National Tourism Week). It also helped to have a celebrity speaker for the opening, keynote address. Keep in mind that television coverage more than any other media can be very capricious. I don't delude myself. If a shooting occurred nearby during my event, I would have lost the camera crews in a heartbeat.

There are two other approaches you should consider for local coverage. The first is to be aware of and familiar with every single local news show. Watch them to develop a sense of what kinds of guests appear. Try to tailor the reasons you're seeking publicity with the type of television show. For example, if your idea deals with business, it's obvious that you should look for shows that have business-related guests. If the show is more feature-driven and you have a business idea, the struggle that you went through should be the angle you push. Another idea to pitch is how what you did (or do) will affect the consumer.

Another approach is less common but also works. By pitching a story now, television stations might film the story but use it later. Sometimes a station will send out a crew (often young interns on weekends, depending on the size of the market) for a story they know the station will address in the future. I have a client which is a major utility company that's traded on the New York Stock Exchange. I'm responsible for publicizing a division that offers contracting services which include air-conditioning, heating and plumbing expertise. When we sent out a media alert and tip sheets, we talked about how consumers could 1) run their air conditioners more efficiently; 2) save money; 3) get more knowledge about choosing an HVACR contractor. A TV news assistant called, and we arranged an interview and "shoot." This means that in early July, the weather was not exceptionally hot that weekend, but the station knew that sooner or later the temperature would again climb into the hot zone. The station also knew it would need file film when it aired stories about the hot weather. They can air this file film at a moment's notice. In the magazine business, we label these types of feature stories as evergreens, which means that the article is essentially always "fresh" because you can use it any time.

Creating Your Own Television Show. A word about public access channels. While rules vary among communities, the object is to provide a forum for local citizens to air their opinions. Depending on the nature of your business, this can be an extremely fruitful venture for local publicity and a strong weapon in promoting yourself beyond your geographic confines. The key is that often you must produce your own show, which means you have to pick up the tab for production. (This can run into hundreds if not thousands of dollars.) Also, broadcasting rules forbid overt commercialism. How much publicity you can generate depends on your local stations' interpretation of commercialism and your own savviness in promoting yourself without using a sledgehammer. Here's how to begin.

Call your local cable station and ask what are the rules and regulations about public access. Ask them to send you the information that explains their policies. Ask if they have a course or seminar that walks you through the steps of starting your own program. In some instances, such as in Cleveland, the local community college would actually allow residents to use their studio for taping purposes, providing you book it far enough in advance. It is a marvelous opportunity for cable access without the hurdle of expense, time and talent. The one requirement in Cleveland, as I recall, was that you had to attend a one-evening seminar on cable access, which cost a one-time fee of about $10.

Let's go back to the restaurant business as an example. Let's say that you're in the restaurant business and your specialty is Italian cooking. Why not do a show on Italian cooking? You could easily put together one or two shows each month where you explain one of your recipes. You can't publicize your restaurant like an advertisement, but nothing prevents you from wearing a chef's apron with the words, "Luigi's Place," or during your demonstration patter, you say occasionally, "At Luigi's, we like to . . ." The rule is simple. Most people know when you're pushing a product, which is fine, and they also know when it becomes too loud, insistent and too repetitive. Use common sense.

Now you're on cable television every weekday and you're making local inroads. What's next? Well, if you're really good, it means that you have a depth of cooking knowledge and you're constantly working on improving your television presentation. This is important – because you shouldn't lower your standards just because you're appearing "only" on a cable channel. Prepare and examine each show as though you had a nationwide audience. Never stop assessing how you present your topic and always look for ways to improve. Watch the best food shows that you enjoy and observe how they do it. You can use the tape to work for you when you're not on television. Send the tape to your banker when you're asking for a loan for the next restaurant or to the cable access station in another community where you're eyeing a new location. Hoping to write a local food column? Send the tape to the editor. It'll show that you're the real thing. In short, it greatly establishes your credibility, one of the great results of positive publicity.

Gimmicks. Some people are really good at gimmicks and publicity. I'm not, probably because I've been a journalist for too long and also because gimmicks, as a rule, cost money, and I *hate* to spend my clients' money. (Isn't that the whole point of this book: free publicity?)

However, this is one instance where gimmicks seem to work in the radio and television world of journalism. (As a general rule, do NOT try this with newspaper people. It is probably OK to try it with magazines, too.) I'm not going to explain why television and radio in particular find this acceptable and most newspapers don't. Maybe it's because broadcast knows (no matter what they say) that they're in the entertainment business. Newspapers don't. I will only add that using gimmicks with press releases occurs far more frequently in the broadcast world compared to the print world.

Often people send a press release to broadcast media accompanied by a "gift." Now, this is not outright bribery (in most cases) but it is an attempt to break from the pack and gain attention for your publicity goals. Often it takes the shape of food, trinkets or books (authors, keep this in mind).

Here's how it works. You take the press release and deliver it (or have someone else do it) directly to the television studio or radio station. Be sure you know precisely who should receive it and also make sure that is the person who decides whether to assign coverage for your story.

Try to keep to a theme with the press release. If you want to publicize a Latino festival by your church, send a hot, steamy, delicious plate(s) of Latino food to various members of the stations. (You might have to feed several people.) If it's lunch food, make sure someone delivers it by 11:15 a.m., before the noon broadcast and before they order out. Anything works, but the more creative you are, the more likely you are to get attention. You can send flowers, candy, doughnuts, books, puzzles, toys (if you know the producer or host has children), tickets to your event. (I would NOT send tickets to some other event, such as a rock concert. People might regard that as a bribe. Nor would I send a Rolex watch.) What you're sending is a friendly gesture, and, yes, it's all in the interpretation. I once got movie tickets AFTER I wrote a complimentary profile about a businessperson. After mentioning it to my editor, I sent a thank-you note and returned the tickets. You can't go wrong with food and trinkets.

When we used this technique to promote a Midwestern city that was "hot" as a tourism destination, we put Red Hots candy, suntan lotion, sunglasses and similar items in a gift bag tied to a balloon. The theme was that our city was "hot."

Tom's Tips:

- No matter what you send, if your request for coverage is a dud, you won't get a newsperson to cover your event or story idea. It must have news or entertainment value.
- If you want to publicize the event, you can send it the day of the event (unless it's very early in the morning) or the day before. I would generally send it the day before so that they can put it in the news budget for the next day.
- Food is always great, especially for morning programs. Imagine the radio station getting a dozen bagels, two or three different kinds of cream cheese and a pot of coffee. Use your imagination and some creativity. The more off the wall, the greater the impact and fun you'll have.

Tom's Tip: Let's say that you've decided a local TV talk show would be really important to your publicity efforts. Let's also say you're a clothes designer with mostly local clients, and that's why this show is so important to you. How would the Big T (that's me) do it? Here's how.

First, I'd watch the show for a week or two to get familiar with the host or hostess' style and the type of guests that appear.

Second, I'd send them breakfast food every Monday for a month. But before I'd send them the breakfast food, I'd call the switchboard when it opened and tell the receptionist that I wanted to send Kathy Smith some bagels and coffee and ask if she has any preferences. I'd also ask if the studio had breakfast food available. (Many larger studios have food on the premises for their guests.) If they did, I'd scratch the idea of bagels but maybe go with something else like homemade pies.

Third, I'd include a tantalizing press release without telling her what I wanted. I would say that I've got a great idea for her (the hostess' audience) and will pitch it in the near future.

Fourth, I'd keep this up for three, maybe four weeks with a tease each time.

Fifth, I'd finally include a media kit about myself and a press release announcing something about my line as a designer (both from a business and personal perspective), and I would offer to have members of the staff act as models for my clothes.

Do I know 100 percent guaranteed that this approach would work? No. I put the smart money on myself, though. Notice in the final pitch, it's still a terrific story idea, an excellent visual (you could also pre-select audience members, but sizing could be an issue) and you've piqued the host's (or producer's) curiosity. You get on the show (of course, you're having a professional taping service provide you with a copy). For a total cost of maybe $100, you have a shot at appearing on the top, local television show. [If it fails, go to the No. 2 show on your list.] If television is important to your publicity efforts, it takes creativity, a good idea with promising visuals, timing and good luck to get on the air. Appearing on television can give you instant star appeal and recognition, even if it's only momentary.

A few thoughts about television.

Television is the first truly democratic culture – the first culture available to everyone and entirely governed by what the people want. The most terrifying thing is what people do want.
Clive Barnes, critic

One of television's great contributions is that it brought murder back into the home, where it belongs.
Alfred Hitchcock, movie director

Chapter 26

Public Speaking

"A Good Speech Is Like A Sharpened Pencil; It Has A Point."

I looked forward to writing this chapter. My favorite quote (which is my own) is, "Most journalists are social maladroits." Of course, that's a bit harsh and filled with hyperbole, but many journalists write better than they speak. Surprise, huh? That's why they became journalists. I'd also say that journalists are the worst joiners. They join nothing. I remember a series of advertisements – either in the *Columbia Journalism Review* or the *American Journalism Review* – which sought journalists to join the National Press Club in Washington, D.C. They appealed to these potential members – journalists for the most part – as people who didn't join anything. I was glad to see these pillars of the journalism profession confirm my unofficial assessment.

What does this have to do with public speaking? Because I fit the profile of most journalists when it comes to joining, it says a lot about why I joined Toastmasters, which keeps me in speaking trim for the lectern circuit. If you enjoy talking to people, if you enjoy addressing the public and professional groups, this is one of the best ways of promoting yourself. Yes, it's one small step at a time because it's unlikely you will be speaking in front of hundreds or thousands of people within a few months. It's the target audience that matters and not the size. [For example, if you're a financial planner, in an industry that appears to have everyone jostling each other to get out and talk to groups, you already know the drill.] A financial consultant invites you to a free dinner and the opportunity to attend a financial planning seminar (read sales pitch). Competition is tough. I've talked to radio station producers, and financial planners deluge them with requests to appear as experts (ho-hum, what else is new). Now, for the record, I have nothing against financial planners. I know some who are terrific people. It is an industry, however, where the word HAS gotten out that they should speak to groups. Financial planners already recognize the value of selling their products by using effective publicity tactics, especially as public speakers. (This is not to say that they are effective public speakers, but that's another issue.)

Test time. If you're so smart, Tom, how would you advise a financial planner? Here's one approach. First, you probably should decide on a niche market. For our purposes, we'll choose people who fit this criteria: 1) people over 50; 2) those who haven't saved anything yet. (I personally think this is a large, untapped market.) Now you must do two things: You prepare a speech or presentation to this group. When you're sure that you can deliver it, you prepare to find groups that fit this category. We're going under the assumption that you haven't written a book (which makes my job much easier). Do you also see the difficulty I created with my scenario? Are you really going to give advice to people, saying to them, "you're a financial loser because you're 50 and haven't saved anything"? And yet, that's precisely the group that you want because some will make money, they really do need your advice, it's a large market, and by 50 if they're not serious about saving and financial planning, they probably never will be (unless you can convince them to change). Contacting this group presents a challenge, but reaching them is crucial to your success. Also, you have the added component that when you find (or reach) them, you can't come right out and say they're financial misfits. After all, would you go to a speech or presentation when you knew everyone attending was a financial failure? I would create a list of every group in my area that might have some members of the category for which I'm looking and reach them with a small direct-mail campaign. I would repeat that mailing at least three or four times each year. For example, my town has a local chapter of the AARP. They would be an obvious target. (Be sure to find out who the decision maker of the group is and write to that person directly. Then, follow up with a call.) I would look for opportunities to write for local publications, the smaller the better. I would really zero in on publications that focus on middle-age or senior readers. In my tagline, I would stress my availability to speak to groups about financial planning for people over 50. I would conduct the same approach for local radio, again pushing the issue of speaking for free to a group of people 50+. How to handle the "loser" image I mentioned earlier? It's a matter of wording and positioning. I would couch my approach in terms of "Securing Your Financial Future After 50."

The real story on how to get speaking engagements. EVERY book I've ever read about publicity and marketing repeats the advice to go out and talk to groups to get practice speaking so that you can improve your message and become more proficient at selling yourself as an expert. I love that advice because it's so good. They'll tell you to talk to your church and service organizations like the Lions or Moose. **THIS ADVICE IS ALSO OFTEN MEANINGLESS**. Let me explain. When I moved to New Jersey, I sent out 350 letters offering my services as a FREE public speaker. I offered to give tips to the organizations about how to get free publicity. Now, while these organizations might not want profit in the same manner as a business person, they certainly need to attract new members, retain current members, reignite fallen-away members, and often, they NEED TO RAISE MONEY for their organization. I included a terrific letter, the list used for the mailing was "fresh", I included my credentials and I sent the mailing first-class so it wouldn't look like junk mail.

I received three inquiries. That's it. One came from a public relations person who really wanted career advice, another person thought he might have me address his group (but never could make up his mind), and the third resulted in a speech to the Lions Club in Maple Shade, N.J. (nice group).

When I did the same type of mailing for a client in the HVAC industry (Heating, Ventilation and Air Conditioning), we didn't receive a single acceptance on his offer to talk about how to stay cool in the summer, save energy and reduce costs. We didn't get one hit. Not one! And I timed this mailing to coincide with summertime when the temperatures were soaring.

Now I know what you're thinking (especially if you're engaged in public relations or advertising). You'll say the mailing list was not fresh. It was current, and I personally had someone compile it. A lot of time and money.

Then you'll say, well, maybe the copy I sent wasn't that good. Maybe it wasn't *compelling* enough. Now I know something about writing copy, and the copy was someplace between good and really good. I've had successful campaigns in the past, so why shouldn't this one succeed? In both instances, the results were dreadful compared to my usual standards for success. Besides, we're talking about FREE, for crying out loud. People love that word.

Does that mean, don't bother offering to speak for free to social service organizations or other like organizations?

A True Story. A few years ago, I had lunch with the former president of the National Speakers Association (NSA), who charged, at the time, $8,000 for a single speech. He told me that his speaking career kicked off when a secretary sent out a flier to various groups in the area offering his services as a free speaker on some psychology-related topic (he was a shrink). Good grief, this was a flier that his secretary cooked up (no disrespect to secretaries). How could he possibly get more engagements than me? I'm the publicity expert. Several organizations called him, asking him to speak. He became better known and slowly began to speak more frequently. Finally, the speaking became so lucrative that he gave up the shrink business – he has a Ph.D. in psychology – and hit the road as a highly paid speaker. (He also writes books – no surprise.)

So what works and what doesn't? Who knows? Actually, I think there is an answer. The difference between my campaign and his was the topic. He made people care about what he was going to talk about, and I didn't convince my audience that the topics I would deliver, or my client's, really mattered or seemed that interesting. I also neglected to repeat the mailing a few times.

So what should you do? Write a one-page letter explaining what you would like to talk about. Think of every group that might find your topic interesting. Better yet, find groups that **need** your information and send that information (letter or flier) to every organization within the driving radius that you would consider acceptable. (I mailed to every group in my county and the two adjoining counties.) Then, follow up with a phone call if you're reasonably sure that the group is important to you as a potential client or customer.

Tom's Tip: Conduct this at least several times each year, but if you do it only once a year, be sure to conduct a mailing at the same time each year for one simple, but critically important, reason. Organizations change officers each year, and the incoming officer might be interested in your talk, whereas the former officer could not care less.

If you obtain a speaking engagement, BE SURE TO LEAVE SOMETHING WITH THE AUDIENCE THAT IDENTIFIES WHO YOU ARE, WHAT YOU DO AND, MOST IMPORTANT, HOW TO CONTACT YOU.

The dumbest thing you can do is to make this great effort and then not have a handout. It doesn't have to be blatant. If you're a model train expert, why not have a one- or two-page sheet explaining the three most popular model trains? Include your business's pertinent information at the top of the handout. Talk to whomever is interested in speaking with you afterwards. Be sure to pass out business cards to everyone who saunters by.

How Do I Prepare For Those Speeches I'm Going To Give? Now for the joining part. Unless you're a natural, the best and least-expensive way to improve your public speaking is to join Toastmasters. You can find the nearest club at www.toastmasters.org or simply look in the White Pages under Toastmasters. Often there's a listing. I'm a member of a chapter in southern New Jersey (and remember, I don't join anything), and it's been a great experience. The dues are minimal, and it gives you great practice and feedback on your speaking. Also, because I teach *Publicity For Profit* seminars, I wanted to be sure that I was as effective as possible and also wanted to reduce or eliminate any speaking approach that was distracting, irritating, ineffective or confusing. Toastmasters clubs are great forums to practice your speaking skills. Dale Carnegie courses are excellent ways to learn public speaking too, but they're expensive. If your company or organization pays for it, then go for it. I believe the current price is at least $1,000. The only problem is that after you've taken the course, you must continue to practice what you've learned. That's why many graduates of Dale Carnegie join Toastmasters. Public speaking is similar to any skill; if you don't hone the skill on a regular basis, it begins to deteriorate.

Public speaking also is a terrific venue for an audience, presumably one that you wish to influence, to judge you, your product or your service. You have the advantage of being an expert by the very act of appearing on the speaking platform. Initially, you might speak for free. Eventually, someone might even **pay** you to speak. Now that's really getting the publicity momentum moving in the right direction. You get to promote your message and get the publicity that accompanies all speakers. That means you're in the company or organization's communications package (press release, newsletter, convention guide, Web site), which gives potential attendees information about you and your topic.

Public speaking allows you a powerful four-way approach to publicity.

First, you have an audience and the publicity that comes with giving a presentation. Second, you have the opportunity to sell whatever it is that you want the publicity for, to an audience that you deemed important. Third, if you become proficient, someone might actually pay you to speak while you're promoting your own business (isn't that a stunning thought?). Finally, you might get new customers or clients from the audience or additional speaking engagements.

Tom's Tips:

Practice. If you simply hate to get up in front of an audience because your throat becomes constricted, your knees shake and you become uncontrollably lightheaded, then public speaking might be too much of an obstacle to overcome. However, virtually everyone who takes a stab at public speaking is adequate at best when they begin. With <u>regular</u> practice, a cordial atmosphere and the gentle feedback of Toastmasters, you *will* improve. I absolutely, positively guarantee this. Remember my comments that if you could write simple sentences and string them together, you have the ability to become a published author? This applies to public speaking, too. I remember talking to a friend of mine who is an excellent speaker with whom I've shared the platform. We talked about this issue, and I mentioned my view (similar to my views on writing) that most people had the capability to give anywhere from an adequate to an articulate presentation if they just made the effort. His comment on public speaking was telling: "Americans just don't like to practice." I never forgot that.

This simply means that most of us are not born speakers, we train ourselves into becoming one. Keep practicing.

Leave-behind. Never, ever, speak to a group without having a "leave-behind" that gives people some valuable information. In that information, always include your name, address, phone number, e-mail address and web page if you have one. I'm still astonished when I see a public speaker break this rule. (Unless, of course, you don't want the audience to contact you.) And try as hard as possible NOT to allow ANYONE to leave the room without information about you, your product or service.

Provide an introduction. Whenever you speak, always have someone introduce you. Write the introduction yourself and fax or e-mail it to the person who will give the introduction and ask them to read it. These people will appreciate the fact that you've made their job easier and are in control by providing an introduction that is most beneficial to you. Keep it short, no longer than two or three paragraphs. (Don't forget to bring a copy to the speaking venue, because about half the time, the person introducing you will have lost or misplaced the copy you sent.) Always include in the introduction that you'll be available to meet for a few minutes with anyone after the presentation if the circumstances allow.

Selling yourself, your ideas or your expertise. DON'T GIVE A PRESENTATION THAT TURNS INTO A NONSTOP COMMERCIAL FOR YOUR PRODUCT OR SERVICE. An example of this is sharing information and then mentioning countless times that the "real" information is in a book or tape you produced or a seminar that you teach. You are cheating the audience. You will also infuriate them and the person who hired or asked you to speak.

Offer to speak for free. Now that you've heard both sides of the discussion that deals with the effectiveness of offering your speaking services for free, should you make the effort? Absolutely. Just don't be lulled into thinking that people will knock down the door to accept your offer. It might start slowly, but it's a start, and you will receive some offers <u>if you persist</u>. I offered to speak for free when I started out. I consider the assignments that I gained to be practice. Don't forget this important fact: **When I spoke for free, I provided the organization and audience the same standard of excellence that I demand of myself for a paying audience. There is no difference.** Now, of course, you must pay to hear me speak. (My advice on getting published which I discussed earlier, for example, started out many years ago in a class I taught for **free**, to would-be writers. You will always learn from this experience. When you're offering to speak for free, be sure to mention that you'll be happy to accommodate them on short notice if possible. This will help attract speaking engagements. It's how I received my first invitation to speak. They were thrilled that I could "fill in".)

Speak at every opportunity. Whether it's your church or synagogue's library committee, the PTA or the dinner for your daughter's baseball team, never pass up the opportunity to get up in front of an audience. I'm not saying hog the show, I'm only advising that you share a few moments. It's wonderful practice, and you'll not only get better, you'll be happy you did it.

Tom's Tip: After you start to speak, guess what? You became an expert on speaking. A few days ago, I became aware of a journalist writing an article about giving the toast as the best man at a wedding. She was looking for tips. I literally knocked out about five or six suggestions about giving a toast and e-mailed them to her. My credentials: 1) I wrote a book on publicity, which makes me an expert on communications; 2) I had given a toast as a best man at several weddings; 3) I was a member of Toastmasters and for a project actually had to give a "toast"; 4) As a public speaker, I know something about giving toasts (after all, no matter how you define it, it is public speaking). The journalist replied that future best men would thank me for my tips. She was going to use every tip I submitted. As I'm fond of saying, I actually follow my own tips on publicity.

A True Story. After sending out a letter and a one-page info sheet on my speaking topic for my first attempt at public speaking for free, the public relations head of a Lions club called and asked if I could speak at their next meeting (about three days away). Since the evening was open, I said yes, and she was ecstatic because all this person needed was a warm body. Me. The evening started with cocktails, dinner and then my speech. I spoke for 30 minutes (10 minutes too long), and I became far too technical and gushed with too much information during my allotted time span. Sometimes my enthusiasm is a weakness. They didn't throw food at me, and only a few people snoozed. The lesson here was that I should have focused only on one or two points about publicity and shared more interesting stories. I forgot a basic rule and won't make that mistake again. While I no longer speak for free, I will donate my time to a small group of charities where I live. Either way, I do it because I like the rush of being at the lectern and I enjoy, even more, seeing someone's eyes light up when they understand some lesson I'm trying to impart. It's really that simple: Speak and earn publicity.

Chapter 27

Teach A Course

"Listen Up, Class!"

"There's no word in the language I revere more than teacher. None. My heart sings when a kid refers to me as his teacher and it always has. I've honored myself and the entire family of man by becoming one."
– Pat Conroy, Prince of Tides

Becoming a teacher is not the usual approach one conjures up when thinking of ways to get free publicity. Teaching a course actually gives you visibility in two areas. First, you have the captive audience in your class. (This mimics the influence of publicity when you're behind the lectern as a public speaker.) If the audience is a potential target for people who you wish to influence, you gain the automatic aura of the expert. There is a presumption that by being in front of a class, you must know what you're talking about. It's no accident that many professions suggest that members of their industry teach a course to get leads or potential customers. Returning to my financial planners example, they realize that the "secure" structure of a class, the implicit trust factor which a teacher enjoys and the access to potential clients are a dynamite combination. If you have a restaurateur teach a cooking class, wouldn't it seem logical that at some point a trip to her restaurant is mandatory?

But this is only part of the story. Where publicity becomes really broad is the attention and free press coverage you gain as part of the school or institution's advertising campaign to attract students. Inevitably, they list the classes that are available, often with the names of the teachers and sometimes their background.

A True Story: Believe it or not, since the beginning of my business, I've never felt the need to use a public relations campaign because, as a one-person operation, I've always had enough referrals to keep me busy. I didn't want to hire any employees to handle the excess offers thrown my way. (My attitude on this issue changed once I had a few associates and wrote a book.) But partially in fun and partially as a way to practice my public-speaking ability, I decided to teach a course. In my area, there was an organization called the Learning Studio (with five locations), which had wonderful facilities. I also noticed that a local community college and my small town offered classes through an adult education program. So I went after all three. I ended up teaching at the Learning Studio and the community college. The local adult education program was recalcitrant about getting back to me, though if I had been more aggressive, I'm sure they would have found a slot for me. (Eventually they did. A year later, they called back, and now I teach two classes in my hometown.) My primary two choices decided to sponsor my class, and that was enough. Now where's the PR? In the case of the Learning Studio, they issue a catalog about nine times each year and print about 40,000 copies per issue. In each catalog, I had a description of my Publicity For Profit seminar, my photo and a small bio about myself. "That's 360,000 impressions," as they like to say in the business. I don't know the exact count of the catalog that my community college sends out, but I know it's in the tens of thousands.

The beautiful part about teaching is that most of these schools don't require a large number of students to enroll before they offer a class. A minimum number usually suffices. That means, with any luck and a little pizzazz, when you write the copy to attract students, the school will make your course a permanent fixture in its catalog. By now, you know how I enjoy repetitive, no-cost publicity that goes on autopilot once you've done the groundwork. Teaching a class is one of those low-cost, repetitive publicity campaigns that can go on and on. I know people who've been teaching classes for years.

The other element to this publicity approach is that the school pays you while they help promote your expertise with free publicity. Now that's a novelty. A terrific combination: pay AND free publicity.

But in order to use the publicity associated with teaching most effectively, you must follow some rules if you want to extract the maximum benefit of obtaining media coverage.

Tom's Tips:

- Decide what kind of course you will teach and how broad or narrow it should be. For example, let's say you want to teach a course on marketing. That's a large pill to offer and an even larger one for people to swallow. I'm not saying you can't do it, but it's very broad. I would suspect that a course on the basics of marketing on the Internet would be a more focused choice.
- Decide where you want to teach. Do you want to teach at an independent learning school, an adult education program sponsored by your local community or an accredited two- or four-year college? I've never been interested in teaching a college course that runs from eight to 12 weeks. I simply don't have the time. I've always favored a seminar-length course for a few hours over one evening or two at the most. Again, I frame my schedule this way because of my time constraints. Indeed, my one-night courses were the training ground and practice runs for my Publicity For Profit seminars. Be sure that after making the commitment, your follow-through is impeccable. You must deliver the goods.

- Call the college or teaching institution and ask for the office that is responsible for adult education teachers. When you get the right person, ask what you should send them to propose a course. Be sure to look at the most recent catalog BEFORE you suggest a course. Obviously, you shouldn't suggest a course if the school already offers it, unless you have a different angle on the subject so that it doesn't appear repetitive. (When I first called the Learning Studio, the person with whom I spoke gave me this advice.) I replied by saying that I wouldn't have made the phone call without ensuring that my proposed course did not mimic a similar course. Her reply: "You'd be amazed at how many people call me about teaching a course without ever looking at our catalog." In truth, there was a marketing course that certainly covered several aspects of what I teach. I just made sure that there were enough different aspects in my course to warrant a separate class.
- Send the school an information packet that contains the following in this order:
  1. The Warm Up. A brief letter offering to teach a course.
  2. The Sales Pitch. A one-half to one-page information sheet explaining who should take the course, what the course is about, what students will learn and how they will benefit from the course.
  3. Who Are You? Submit a biography of yourself. You must answer this basic question: Why are you qualified to teach this course? Tip: This is not the time for modesty.
  4. Write It Yourself. Include a short, one-paragraph course description the school can include in its catalog. Don't have them write it, you write it. Make their job easier. In the course description, make sure you completely identify yourself and give the reader a chance to contact you if they wish. An example: The instructor, T.S. Peric', president of Cherry Hill,

NJ-based Galileo Communications Inc., has gained millions of dollars worth of free publicity for his clients.

5. Lights, Camera, Action. If the catalog allows photos, be sure to include a professional photo of yourself. Those 360,000 impressions I mentioned earlier – included my photo.
6. Boost The Bio. Include anything else that you might think will solidify yourself as an expert. In my case, I sent copies of various magazines for which I've served as editor (it carries my photo in the editor's column). In short, remove your name from the pile of other wannabe teachers. I buttressed my claims to my expertise and separated myself from competitors by extolling my expertise about the media, proving that I've been a member of the fourth estate.
7. Request Face Time. Ask for an appointment to meet the person who decides, if that's possible. You must be persistent in following up. When I went to the Learning Studio, my contact waved in the direction of a large pile of mail and pointed directly to an oversized, white-manila envelope. She said: "I got those three months ago and need to get back to them." Why was she interviewing me when she had a backlog of three months' worth of queries for teaching positions? I separated myself from the pack by showing up unannounced, wearing a suit with a briefcase in hand. (This is not the way I usually dress for the office, which means I had to dress up "special" that day.) I wanted her to know I was serious. I think she got the message.
8. Testing Your Teaching. If you gain an interview to teach a class, be prepared, whether it's stated or not, to "teach" your course. They might not tell you, but the interview is a brief classroom session for the school to observe you. I gave a 15-minute presentation to the person who interviewed me at

the Learning Studio so that she would have a sense of my knowledge, teaching style and speaking ability. If you get an interview, offer to give a short presentation, even if they haven't asked for it. (I'm assuming here that you're confident about your ability to deliver an enthusiastic, well-organized, abbreviated classroom session.)

9. Hand Out Handouts To Your Students. As always, never forget the "leave behind." Remember: Always make it as easy as possible for people to contact you.

A True Story: I had lunch with a former president of the National Speakers Association, and I asked him what was his most potent marketing device. I was stunned at the answer. He said: "My business card." He gives a business card to EVERYONE. He has passed out tens of thousands during the past decade. This resulted in more referrals for speaking engagements (he was up to $8,000 per speech when we spoke) than any other form of marketing or public relations. Stunning. The business card is the most ubiquitous, least-thought-of "leave behind". Never, ever leave home or the office without it. Give it to everyone, even that gangling 18-year-old teenager. He or she just might own a television station one day.

Tom's Tip: This actually came from Sharon Nittinger, a fellow toastmaster who applied it so masterfully. She wanted advice about teaching, so we met for coffee one morning, and I shared with her essentially the same points in this chapter. The local adult education school and a local community college accepted Sharon's offer for teaching a class (the same ones to which I forwarded my offer). Then, Sharon went one step better. With the local adult education program, she offered TWO classes. The program director gave her the green light for both! So, if you feel really confident and know the classes are not too similar, you might want to give this a try. My advice on this issue: If you've never done any teaching or speaking in front of a group, restrict it to one session for the first time unless, of course, you have boundless confidence. Sharon, I must add, is an extremely good speaker and a professional trainer. She can speak better publicly, half asleep, than many people can totally awake.

A True Story: Remember the local adult school that never got back to me (which I mentioned earlier)? The same program that brought on Sharon for TWO classes? Well, the director called me about two weeks ago and said, "I saw you mentioned in the Learning Studio catalog, and I still have your material. You wouldn't be interested in teaching at our program, would you?" Naturally, I said yes, but I added: "I have another course in addition to '*Publicity For Profit*.' I just wrote a book and now I can offer a course called, 'How To Write A Book.' Her reply: "They'll love this course." So now I have two courses to teach in the fall. What's really interesting is that the director kept my information for more than a year. By getting my course advertised in a competing catalog that offered programs (the publicity factor), I reaffirmed the idea that my seminar had value. I love stuff like this. (Don't forget those press releases announcing your classes!)

The last word on teaching. I shouldn't have to say this, but I will. Just like in public speaking, you MUST give value, which means you must share valuable and useful information. Again, you CANNOT use a class as a springboard to sign them up for a more-expensive version of some other product or service. That's ethically dishonest, and you'll only anger your audience. As I always recommend, use common sense. People don't care if you promote your product or service as long as it's a small part of the overall class. Here's how I do it for my seminars.

When I begin, I tell the group that we have a two-hour session. I tell them that I'm going to instruct them for 118 minutes and then would like to spend two minutes promoting my book. Then I ASK them if it's OK? No one has said no so far. Then I ask for a volunteer, and I give her a one-minute egg timer (in the shape of an hourglass filled with sand) and ask her to hold on to it until the end of the class. When it comes to the final two minutes, I begin the pitch for my book (or consulting services). Before I do so, I let the class know that my volunteer is using that one-minute egg timer as a clock. When two minutes are done, I stop and shut up. It works for me.

I love to teach. My first professional job was teaching (even before I went to college). That may be why I feel so comfortable in front of a group that is interested in learning about a topic that makes their lives more interesting, easier or just plain enriching. If you feel the same way, combining teaching and publicity leaves you with a glow of achievement and a very effective way to gain publicity.

Chapter 28

Becoming A Source

Take Note Of This Important Chapter

A byproduct of being a good journalist is that you're always chewing over possible story ideas. You're either wishing that you had the time to chase down a story and write it or wondering why you never read a story that's begging to be written but which you don't have the time to write or you don't work for a publication in which it can appear. (Here's an example: I've never read an article that tracked down the direct descendents of really famous people. I don't mean going back 100 years. I'm thinking of 200, 300, even 500 years ago, assuming it's possible. Whatever happened to the Isaac Newton or Galileo family line? Is there a direct descendent of Charles "The Hammer" Martel? (He's the guy who whipped the Moors at The Battle of Tours for those of you who are historically impaired. Not the cognac.)

The point is that superior journalists always look for good news stories. I constantly give news people ideas for potential stories that have absolutely NOTHING to do with my clients. It's just a good news story. I'm also blunt about saying, "Hey, Joe, I think this could make a great article, and I'm not connected to the people in ANY way. They are not clients, but I thought you might be interested." A note like this works wonders over a period of time even though the reporter or editor knows that you're trading. You're giving them ideas today that are (hopefully) really interesting, for their attention in the future when you pitch a story that might have some self-interest involved, such as your client's involvement in a project. Does this buy any guarantee for future coverage? Of course not, unless the journalist is unethical. What you have created are a bond and a huge dose of goodwill (and respect) with the journalist with whom you're sharing ideas. An editor of one of America's larger newspapers told my wife that I was very good at my job. Sure, I had lunch with him a few times, and we chatted about each other's background, but none of that should have resulted in such a positive remark. Possibly, he based his comments on basic politeness to my wife, because, how does he really *know* that I'm good? Here's what he did know. On a somewhat regular basis, I would send him story ideas. I didn't expect him to act on all of my ideas. I only wanted him to recognize: 1) I knew a good story idea when I spotted one; 2) I was willing to share the idea with him exclusively; 3) I demonstrated my fair-mindedness by NOT having a client involved.

In short, I wanted to establish that I understood his job and for him to know that I appreciated the demands he faced on a daily basis, which include part of the foundation for all good journalism: good story ideas. (Good reporting and writing are the other two elements that reporters and editors face every day. However, they are both outside of my control because they're internal, unique to the newsroom. But, I can contribute to the flow of story ideas and have an impact.)

What kind of ideas did I send him? I recall stopping at a traffic light and seeing several well-dressed, polite African-Americans selling products such as beads and perfume, right from the curb. While they would speak to drivers at the traffic light, they were never intrusive and never gave the impression that they were either giving a hard sell or acting in any kind of aggressive manner. I rather liked this entrepreneurial spark and thought, wouldn't it be great to give these young (mid-20s) business people a plug in the newspaper. (My confession: As the business editor on a daily newspaper, I've always had a soft spot for "small" business people. I'd like to add that I know small-business people who are worth millions.) When I returned to my office, I called this editor and left him a brief voice mail, explaining what I saw and why I thought this was a good story. In this case, I didn't have to tell him that these young fellows were not clients. I would repeat this approach probably every month or two.

Tom's Tip: Here's how I'd conduct this tactic of cultivating reporters or editors with a note or phone calls.

Step One: I would target the most important or several of the most important publications that are vital to my publicity goals. I'd choose the one person at a magazine or newspaper who could have an impact on obtaining coverage for me. (This could also be a radio producer or television newsperson or personality.) Then I'd find out what interested him, especially if he covered a beat, which means an area of specialized interest such as business, politics or lifestyle issues. It's important to focus on a few sources because unless you have unlimited time, you won't really have the opportunity to create a bond with more than one or two journalists.

Step Two: I've always preferred cultivating an editor to a reporter. A characteristic of reporters or writers, who chase down a story, is complete focus, accompanied by frenzied activity associated with the article on which they're working. The last thing they want is to think of the next story. This can make reporters less receptive to thinking about future story ideas.

Also, when dealing with a reporter or writer, you must sell the idea twice: first to the journalist, and then you're betting that the journalist can sell it to the editor. However, if you go directly to the editor and he likes the idea, he'll just assign it, case closed. When I started doing this frequently, I chose the business editor at a major American newspaper

because that's where I was hoping to find publicity for my clients. My client earned millions of dollars in free publicity each year. My mission was to increase those "hits" or the number of exposures. I did it successfully, and this approach – creating contacts based on giving story ideas that had no connection to my clients – helped me get the editor's ear when I wanted it.

Step Three: I also send notes, usually e-mails these days, but handwritten notes, too, to journalists whose stories I really like. I'm especially prone to doing this with *The Wall Street Journal*. I start my day with *The Wall Street Journal* online. (Actually, I start my day with Andrew Tobias' column on *Money and Other Subjects* and then go to *The Wall Street Journal*. Andrew Tobias is the king of personal finance. Find him at www.andrewtobias.com. I love Tobias' column and highly recommend his book, *The Only Investment Guide You'll Ever Need*. I've bought at least five copies and given them to friends. And if you want to learn how to write an ezine (electronic newsletter), no one is better than Tobias. I've read him for years.) Some of you read this and might think I'm pandering to these journalists. Wrong. I only respond when I really think the story or writing (or both) is first class. It's easy to see why these reporters are at *The Wall Street Journal*. Their view is frequently broad and, more importantly, these reporters can often address complex issues with clarity and excellent writing. When I look at the standard of writing and reporting they exhibit, I'm still impressed after all these years; which is probably why some of my friends describe me as a crypto-journalist and not a public relations person. Indeed, it's interesting that I hear so many pejorative comments from public relations people directed towards journalists – in private, of course, or in front of a client ONLY if the client hates the media. Yet these same PR types go on to pitch story ideas to this class of people (journalists) they don't like. (Yes, now a bunch of public relations people will write to me and say that they never participate in this practice nor have they ever heard it done within their office. My reply: I've got pristine, oceanfront property in Florida that I'd like to sell you at a deep discount. Call me and let's work out a price for cash.)

I once sent an e-mail to a *Wall Street Journal* writer (reporters usually reply briefly acknowledging my compliment), and he wrote back that my e-mail was the best he'd received in a long time. For those of you who don't understand journalistic life, this is the reality of the profession: You only (almost) hear about what you didn't do, the slight error you made or the information you left out. You don't hear about how well you wrote or how carefully reported the story was. Nor will you hear about where the real blame lies if there is an inaccuracy because the subject – purposely or by accident – gave you the wrong facts. I remember interviewing a financier (you hear and see his name on public television all the time). He liked the story I wrote about him but offered a slight criticism because I had the wrong number of years he was married. Apparently his wife complained to him. I simply reported what he said. How can I be sure I had correctly reported the information? Because I taped the interview. I had it right. However, I was still wrong in the eyes of him and his wife. Even at *The Wall Street Journal*, story reporters receive very few complimentary notes or letters, especially if you don't count the notes that are thinly disguised efforts at sucking up. I sent a note to a Detroit-based writer at *The Wall Street Journal* complimenting him on the angle and writing of his story. He e-mailed me and said how nice it was to receive a flattering note because he seldom got a compliment. Amazing, isn't it? If reporters at the country's most influential business publication wallow in the shadows of the unknown, imagine what it's like for reporters at your hometown newspaper or magazine. Reporters mostly know that, when it comes to trust, the public rates them not far above used car salesmen.

The most complaints I ever received in my career was as the business editor on a daily newspaper: I failed to mention the name of the high school band that performed at the opening of the (then) largest Kmart store in the world. I took a beating as angry phone calls carpeted the newsroom. Some callers, not surprisingly, suggested a conspiracy. Yes, that's my contribution to the world of conspiracy theory – creating a campaign to smear the high school and its reputation by leaving its name out of a story on the business page. I swear, though, I still can't remember the name of the school.

Tom's Tip: Send a story idea that doesn't benefit you to a journalist. Write a complimentary note to a journalist – some might actually remember your note and name. If not, it's your good deed for the day. Just send a note or make the phone call and compliment a journalist when a story honestly touches you, adds an emotional lift in your daily life or teaches a lesson.

Chapter 29

Take A Tour

"So That's What A Newsroom Looks Like" ...5th Grader

I'm always amazed that people who are interested in publicity never actually go to the media mountain to size it up before the ascent. You're interested in a newspaper or television station and would like to get some coverage but don't have a clue about how they operate. You might not even know from where they operate.

If you're serious about local or regional publicity and you intend to pursue publicity on a regular basis, try getting into the door to develop a sense of the media outlet you want to influence.

If you have a daily newspaper or television station, call them and ask whether they give individual tours. Does this really work? Well, let's find out.

I called the two daily newspapers in my area, the *Courier-Post* and the *Philadelphia Inquirer*, and asked if they give *individual* tours.

Courier-Post. They give group tours. If you're an individual, they will "hook you up" with a group tour.

Philadelphia Inquirer/Philadelphia Daily News. Same rule here. No individual tours, but they will allow you to join a group.

I called just one television station, the NBC affiliate, Channel 10 (Philadelphia). According to the operator, they discontinued tours because of liability issues. Sure. I would pursue this with someone in the news department if I really wanted to see how the newsroom operates.

For a more modest version of this, just walk into your local weekly newspaper or magazine. I'd walk in about 11:50 a.m. and say something to the effect of, "I'd like to talk to an editor about how you accept story ideas." After the introduction, repeat your request, look down at your watch and say, "It's almost lunchtime. Could I buy you lunch and ask you a few questions?" Before you walk in unannounced, be sure to call the publication and ask when is their deadline day. Let's say you walk into a weekly newspaper and find out their deadline day is every Tuesday. That makes it the WORST possible day to contact an editor, let alone stop in unannounced. However, it also gives you a clue about the best day to stop in, which in our example is Wednesday, because as a general rule, most reporters will relax a bit following deadline day. Keep in mind that a monthly publication often considers a week to be "deadline" week. Also, deadline day can change on holiday weeks.

The point of this exercise is important. Unless you're the dullest light around, you will learn something about the news organization in your area or region that you didn't know before you took the tour. I can't tell you exactly what it is, but it'll be something valuable. You might obtain one nugget or several that will tip you off about how and when to pitch your publicity ideas and to whom. What if you met an editor during a tour and he said, "I prefer pitches by telephone but not in the afternoon?" That kind of information is invaluable. (Naturally, when you call to pitch this editor, you would write a tight and bright script and hold it in front of you as you read it.)

The single-biggest problem you will have when pitching an idea – beyond the news value of the idea – is to hold the attention span of the journalist that you're pursuing.

Many people are surprised that reporters, especially those on smaller daily newspapers who write two to four stories each day, get most of their information by phone. They have to because there isn't time to make a personal visit, especially when you might talk with two, three or even more sources for an article. In my journalism days, whenever I personally visited a source, I always learned, saw or heard something I would've missed had I not made that personal visit. Every reporter I know will confirm this. Often we don't do it because of time constraints, but it was and still is the best way to get and assess information. That's why you should make a personal visit.

Tom's Tip: My office is located in Cherry Hill, N.J., and I live in a neighboring town. Recently, I looked at a list of trade magazine editors who I wanted to contact. I e-mailed two, asking them out to lunch. The one in New Jersey declined; the one in New York City accepted. (Both were about one hour and 45 minutes away.) The lunch at an expensive, trendy Chinese restaurant (I paid) turned out to be terrific, because it gave me a firsthand look at how this editor operates. He not only keeps an idea folder (remember me preaching about this) but he does it by the month. Pitch him an idea six months in advance (usually too soon for most magazines) and he'll drop the idea into the appropriate folder. What is the best way to pitch him story ideas? By e-mail. I know because he told me. What else did I learn? We both share a common interest in William Manchester's books on Winston Churchill. He was probably surprised when I told him how terrific the first book was and then whipped it out of my briefcase. (Complete coincidence, but sometimes someone is just smiling on you.)

If you have a regional or even a national media list (as do I), look to see who's local. For me, local is anyone within a two-hour drive if I feel the media outlet is worth the effort.

Once someone meets you, it's much more difficult to be brusque or rude in the future. It's the nice side of becoming a tourist at your more important media outlets. You not only learn what they want, you learn something about them. That makes the hunt for publicity much easier and usually far more civil.

Chapter 30

Publicity And The Internet

The Electronic Age & Publicity – The New Wave

The Internet has created an electrifying, electronic world for people who seek publicity. What makes this particularly interesting is that no one quite knows – no matter what they say – precisely what will be effective or ineffective in the ensuing decade.

But we have already seen the staggering impact of the Internet when used effectively for publicity.

Do you recall the movie, *The Blair Witch Project*? It looks like a movie that your older brother filmed for his sophomore college broadcast journalism class. The movie was about three college kids that allegedly disappeared in the Maryland woods in 1994. It cost a throwaway $35,000 to make and there was certainly little, if any, budget for publicity. Except that the producers used the Internet brilliantly. In June 1998, they published a Web site that for more than one year kept posting information about *The Blair Witch Project*. Between creating verbal buzz and a growing cadre of loyal, young followers who visited the site, the producer firmly anchored the publicity hype before the movie opened. Within three weeks of its opening night, the movie grossed more than $30 million. It was up to $50 million by the end of the summer and resulted in a *Newsweek* cover story that noted: *Blair Witch: Why the Low-Budget Hit Scares Hollywood.* Regardless of the artistic merits of the movie (critics sniffed, the producers strolled to the bank), using the Internet created the information bridge that young people could cross over to before the movie ever had a public viewing.

What does this mean for people seeking publicity? Frankly, it's difficult to give a precise answer except that I have one prediction. As this book goes into future editions, this short chapter will probably become the longest. But let's deal with what we do know, and here are tips for using the Internet for publicity. These include:

- **Get on the Internet**. I hope that everyone who reads this is connected. If not, you risk being irrelevant if you're hoping to get publicity down the road. Yes, traditional methods still work well, but more and more information will migrate to the Internet.
- **E-mail**. No one has the exact numbers, but e-mail is becoming the preferred method of communicating with journalists. I constantly see more and more contact with journalists via e-mail. Many journalists and writers seem to prefer this. This could have a variety of impact including a loss of effectiveness if you have a great sales-type personality when "pitching" your stories. E-mail tends to remove the visible personality factor that helps many people's effectiveness. Writing well in the new Internet style calls for pithy, punchy prose that captures the editor's attention. If you can't get to the point quickly, you're dead.

Tom's Tip: Follow up with the original e-mail. If I send an e-mail to an editor and don't get a reply, I sometimes send the same e-mail a second time (to give him a reminder of the original idea or request) and then repeat my request for action in a different way. What I often do is say something to this effect: "Joe, I haven't heard from you and I didn't want to pitch this idea elsewhere until you had a chance to consider it. If you could give me a quick yes, no, maybe or send more details, I'd be most grateful." (Please do NOT copy my approach. Otherwise we'll all start sounding (writing) alike.) By resending the first e-mail, the editor will be able to see my pitch again, especially if he inadvertently erased it or simply forgot to use it. (For those of you with e-mail, how many times have you simply forgotten to respond to an e-mail, erased it by accident or filed it in an electronic folder and then forgot it?) Now you're asking, why send another e-mail when the lack of a reply should indicate that he's uninterested? Maybe. But when I'm convinced that my story idea or release is right for the journalist, I will sometimes follow up. Another school of thought is that the follow-up e-mail should be DIFFERENT from the first one. This reasoning holds that your pitch should NOT be identical to the first one but rather should push a different angle to your original story. If the editor didn't respond the first time because he was uninterested, sending a similar pitch would doom it to the same fate. But a differently worded pitch might kindle some interest that had not existed before. There is some merit in this thinking.

Tom's Tip: When pitching a story by e-mail, put the headline of your pitch in the subject area. I will sometimes simply write: Story idea. Any editor worth his salt will look to see what the idea is and whether it holds up (is worth pursuing). But you must get to the point **immediately**. Headlines have always been terribly important. Now it is more vital than ever because the editor has less room to scan the first few paragraphs if the headline doesn't work. In other words, in the past, even if the headline was average or mediocre, by scanning down the page, he might see the nugget of an idea that piqued his interest (this happened to me many times). But with the Internet and computer screens, you must physically scroll downward, and often journalists (and other people) won't bother. If you can't write good headlines, get someone who can. It's a talent.

- **Don't send an attachment.** Paste your message or press release right into the text area of the e-mail. Because journalists fear viruses (as do most computer users), they eschew opening any attachment, especially if it comes from someone they don't know. (I confess that I broke this rule early in my Internet days – and still got results – but now I follow the advice I give.) What's the point of sending a tip or release if the editor doesn't read it?
- **Use a signature.** It's easy if you use Microsoft's Outlook Express for your e-mail. A signature is exactly what it says. You sign the e-mail with your name AND vital info such as phone numbers, address, etc. Because I wear different hats for parts of my business, I have SIX different signatures, each legitimate but different to fit the particular circumstances. For example, when I'm sending an e-mail as the editor of one of my magazines, it has my name, the title "editor", the name of the magazine and even my client's e-mail address (something they like me to do). When I sign an e-mail as the writer of this book, it looks like this:
  T.S. Peric', president
  Galileo Communications Inc.
  author of Wacky Days: How To Get Millions
  of $$$ In Free Publicity By Creating
  Your Own Real Holiday & Other Tactics
  Used By Media Experts
  856.874.0049
  856.874.0052 (fax)
  tom@wackydays.com
- **Get a web site.** If you don't have a web site, create one. You need to be current, but here are two reasons related to publicity. If a journalist is interested in something that you send, he might not

bother to call, he might just log on to your web site. If he doesn't find a web site, especially if your story only prompts a borderline case of interest, he might just turn to the next item of interest. Also, if he actually begins writing the story, he'll expect to find at least basic information about your business. Verifying the spelling of a name, address or what you charge for your product is far easier than making a phone call and leaving a message on voice mail and playing phone tag for two days. Consider your web site to be your electronic brochure.

- **Give them what they want.** When you create your initial media list, I presume that you'll send out a hard copy (printed) press release. But DON'T assume. ASK the editor what he prefers. About a year ago, I conducted a random sampling of about 40 editors for a media list I created for a client. Eight responded saying they prefer electronic press releases.
- **Send the electronic version of your press release to the online version of the publication that interests you.** Sometimes the staff of the printed version of a magazine is the same as the online version. And sometimes they're completely different. Find out for your more important publications. When in doubt, send out both versions.
- **New territory**. Online publications or ezines (electronic magazines) like *Slate.com* and *Salon.com* exist which do not have a print counterpart. These publications and electronic newsletters are a great potential market which you won't find in print. Indeed, this market for publicity did not exist before the Internet. It will become increasingly important. Don't ignore online publications which are read by people you want to reach.
- **Consider discussion groups and chat rooms**. Some publicity experts tout visiting these rooms

where people can exchange ideas with the idea that if you establish your expertise, you might get some business or publicity. Maybe. The problem is that this can be very labor-intensive. No one has shown me yet that this works on any regular basis. It's not that I don't think it will work, it's that the time spent to try to make it work in your favor seems too long and laborious. If I'm wrong, let me know.

Tom's Tip: If you go to a chat room, go to where journalists congregate. Find out if there is a forum for pitching ideas.

- **The Web is (almost) instantaneous.** Let's say I want to know about the editorial calendar at a well-known publication. In the old days, I would have to call the publication, and they would mail it to me. At best, they could overnight it. Today, I can jump on the Internet and have the editorial calendar in a matter of minutes. But don't stop at the calendar. Surf a bit to see if they provide writer's guidelines or any other tips about the editorial content of the magazine.

Tom's Tip: Between September and November, most publications publish their editorial calendars. Plan on spending at least a few hours getting the editorial calendars of your more important publications. In some cases, publications also share their editorial guidelines. These are absolute jewels. Imagine having a magazine tell you how to pitch ideas to them!

- **Immediate response.** While you could do it by fax or phone, let's say you're aware of breaking news and immediately make yourself available as an expert because the event relates to your specialty. You could literally write a tip sheet and e-mail it to your 50 journalists (whose e-mail addresses you've carefully collected) in less than 30 minutes.
- **Great rules for pitching ideas to editors.** Go to http://netpress.org/careandfeeding.html for a terrific

roundup article on how to pitch editors using the Internet and what not to do.

- **Tell me!** If you've discovered a successful approach to pitching stories or gaining publicity via the Internet, let me know. I promise you a mention in my book (more free publicity) and a free copy of my next edition. Send it to:

T.S. "Tom" Peric'
2040 Fairfax Avenue
Cherry Hill, NJ 08003
(856-874-0049)
(856-874-0052) fax
tom@wackydays.com

A few thoughts about the Internet and public relations.

The Internet is the first medium that allows anyone with reasonably inexpensive equipment to publish to a wide audience. It is the first medium that distributes information globally at almost no marginal cost.
Bill Gates, CEO of Microsoft Corp.

The rarest of all things in American life is charm. We spend billions every year manufacturing fake charm that goes under the heading of "public relations." Without it, America would be grim indeed.
Anita Loos, U.S. screenwriter, author and humorist

Chapter 31

The Interview

After all this effort, what do you do when a reporter finally calls?

The First Question To Ask When A Reporter Calls.

A True Story. I was teaching a course on publicity, and, in that one-night seminar, there was a lawyer who was clearly struggling to expand his law firm. He had been taking some marketing courses and was now engaged in taking my *Publicity For Profit* seminar. He was a hard guy to read, very little emotion, no enthusiasm. He had a great poker face. I didn't know his exact reason for attending my seminar nor how I could solve his publicity or marketing problems.

I'm sure he was successful, but his business had grown to a logical size. That means that in the manner of how he conducts business, he had peaked. It doesn't mean that the business couldn't grow further. It meant that he had to find a way – a new way – to make the business grow. I commend him for viewing his practice as a business, because many lawyers who fail to understand this distinction often have a practice that doesn't run well as a business. Practicing law has nothing to do with the business of running a law firm. (I have a good friend who is a lawyer who has never gone off on his own, because he recognizes this fact and hates the idea of running a business. He likes the idea of practicing law.) Here I am, teaching this course, sharing all these wonderful tips, and this lawyer mentions at the end of the class that he had a call from a journalist a few days earlier and hadn't returned the phone call. I hope the astonishment on my face wasn't too obvious. What was he doing in my course? He obviously had done something correctly – he had gotten a journalist to call him – and then proceeded to break one of the cardinal rules in hunting for publicity by not returning the journalist's call as soon as possible. What a dummy! This guy not only didn't return the phone call, he probably "burned" this journalist, ensuring that he, the lawyer, would never be used again as a source by that member of the media.

Let me explain how it works. Journalists will often call several people as a source for a story. They will make even more calls if they're on a tight deadline. Guess who the journalist quotes or mentions in the article? The best expert? Not necessarily. The most cooperative expert? Not necessarily. The first person to return the phone call before the deadline? Correct, sir! The person who calls back first with the information or expertise the reporter is seeking is the one most likely to be used in an article. When I wrote stories as a reporter and someone never even bothered to call me back, I rarely called that person again if another "expert" was available. Since few people are the only experts out there in the sea of experts, guess what? I probably don't have to go back to that person. This genius of a lawyer said to me, "Well, I guess I should get back to him." Yeah, maybe you should. And maybe you should keep taking publicity courses, because it sure beats doing the right thing when you have the opportunity.

Here's What You Should Ask. That leads me to this next section about what happens when you actually get a journalist to call you. When a journalist calls, the first question out of your mouth should be: "What is your deadline?"

The journalist's deadline is sacrosanct and, beyond a good story and a great write, this is the ever-present time bomb that is ticking away in his head. Never forget that.

Here are some general rules. Speak now. If you're free to speak when the journalist calls, or even if you're busy, whenever possible, drop what you're doing and let the journalist interview you.

Prepare when you can. If you want to prep yourself with some background information, especially if you have a sense of the direction or reason for the call, asking the journalist what his deadline is helps you determine whether you have the time to brush up on your background and return the call later, while remaining a source for the reporter.

Appreciate the overwhelming demands of deadlines in journalism. If a reporter calls you and he's from a daily newspaper, his deadline is probably tomorrow. That means talk to him NOW or arrange to talk shortly – within a few hours or at his convenience. If the reporter is on a weekly publication, he probably has a few days to deadline. If it's a monthly publication, the journalist probably has a few weeks. You don't know, in the latter two cases, that the journalist didn't wait until the last minute to write the story or began looking for that one, last source (as is often the case). In the case of radio or television news, the deadline is NOW. That means they could be airing your piece by the next news broadcast. That could be minutes away. If it's for the future, they'll tell you because the TV or radio journalist will tape the segment. I simply can't stress too strongly how important deadlines are to journalists. If for some reason you cannot talk immediately, make arrangements to speak as soon as possible, at the convenience of the journalist. Here's what I say: "Bob, I'm just wrapping up a project that will be done in 10 minutes. If you give me your direct number, I promise to call you back without fail in 11 minutes." I've never had this fail me. Of course, I always call back.

Rules of Engagement. "I never said that." "Yes, you did." "No, I didn't."

A True Story: A number of years ago, I was speaking in front of a group of business people along with Jane Bryant Quinn, the nationally syndicated columnist on financial matters. I don't recall the topic that I covered, but for some reason I began talking about the rules of engagement. In short, I tried to explain to this roomful of business types what rules apply when dealing with a journalist. This includes on the record, off the record, on background and not-for-attribution agreements between a source and the journalists.

Quinn followed my presentation, and she contradicted me. She said, in essence, that you should forget all those rules, because you're never going to remember them anyway. Her advice was to simply not say anything that you didn't want to see in print.

Sage advice. She was right, and I was wrong. (I was younger then.)

Unless you deal with the press all the time, you'll never remember the rules. Indeed, the interpretation of those rules varies depending on the relationship between the journalist and subject and even the policies of the news organization.

So let me repeat the sound advice of Ms. Quinn: "When you talk to a journalist, don't say anything that you don't want to see in print." Now this does present a problem. If you become too uptight, you could end up being boring and mechanical. This could minimize your contribution to a story and maybe kill any chance of the journalist using your comments. (I've seen some pretty talkative people get tongue-tied because all of a sudden they were talking to the press.) Conflict, tension, color (idiosyncrasies), storytelling, anecdotes and personal style are just some of the elements in an interview that make it interesting for the journalist and presumably for the reader. Nevertheless, if you have a conviction for smoking pot when you were a kid and now have a respectable business, I'm not sure that you would want to volunteer that piece of information. (Then again, you might want the writer to portray you as an ex-pot-smoking hippy-turned-business-guru.)

An important aside. I love reading books on public relations that want to give you all kinds of coaching about what to say and how to say it. Give me a break! Most of you are going to be exactly who you are. Hopefully, that is a person who has a certain degree of expertise or experience, which is why you're talking to the reporter. It makes sense to infuse your style and speaking manner with a sense of enthusiasm and knowledge. But a personality makeover just for interviews? Get real. Just be yourself. Any coaching will fall by the wayside unless you're talking to the media on a regular basis. So let me repeat the advice. Stay friendly, helpful and enthusiastic but say nothing that will make you wince if you read it.

I can share three pieces of advice which don't require a personality makeover but which will make your interview more effective.

- Be aware of your style. Beware if you pepper your speaking style with lots of asides or extraneous comments or lace it with sarcasm or humor, especially if the reporter conducts the interview over the telephone. This is the only psychologically "mushy" section of this book, meaning you must have some insight into your own personality. Some people, no matter what they believe about themselves, live in a dead zone with regard to their self-awareness. If this is you, none of this will help. For the rest of us, be aware of how you speak. For example, in personal conversations (NOT public speaking), I'm notorious for speaking about one subject and drifting off to another. Often there is a point (and sometimes there isn't), but it can be disconcerting, and unless the listener gives me his rapt attention, he might not see the connection. (Talking about rules of engagement in journalism and then mentioning the Winter War in Finland in 1940 is probably not a wise approach.) Plus, I speak rapidly, which can add to the confusion. When you're on the telephone (the way many print and radio reporters conduct their interviews), be extra careful of using humor or sarcasm which suggests you're joking but which the journalist can't "see". In short, NEVER presume over the telephone. In a face-to-face interview, the reporter might be able to interpret the emotion behind your answer by assessing your gestures, facial expressions or even the tone of how you make a statement. The reporter can see that you're "kidding," but over the telephone, the reporter will take your comments at face value (if you'll forgive the pun).

- Back it up, bubba. If a reporter is following up based on a press release, you had better be prepared to support your statements in the press release. Let's say you claimed to have the fastest pair of hands in the state when it comes to chopping onions. You had better have some supporting documentation such as winning a state championship in that category to prove your claim. There's nothing more disheartening than to actually have a reporter call you and learn that he didn't file (write) the story because you couldn't deliver on the press release or tip sheet that prompted the inquiry. Worse, you've created skepticism in the journalist, who is even less likely to return to you as a source or expert. You've become suspect.
- The most important sentence you'll ever utter. OK, maybe there's a bit of hyperbole here. If you're trying to get free publicity, however, this is the most important sentence you'll ever utter. At some point in an interview, you'll want to create a money quote for yourself. A money quote is a statement of one to three sentences that says what you think is the most

important thing a reader should know about you. (In a sense, it is similar to a Unique Selling Proposition or an elevator speech. Elevator speech? If you're on the sixth floor of a building and you're riding down to the first floor and someone asks, "What do you do?", can you offer a complete if simple answer before the door opens on the first floor? Everyone in sales will tell you that it's necessary to be able to explain what you do in a few succinct sentences.) It really is a good exercise, and, frankly, I've become wary of most people who can't do this. (How do I answer it? "I'm the president of Galileo Communications, which offers editorial and publicity consulting. We also conduct Publicity For Profit seminars which teach businesses and organizations how to obtain thousands of dollars worth of free media publicity.") Is this the best I can do? No. Does it does explain what I do? Yes! I purposely use two sentences (this shows my journalism training) because if I tack on the seminar end of my business, I'm out of breath by the time I've finished, and the listener is out of patience. Has this been effective? It has for me.

In an interview, your money quote might be your elevator speech, but as things change, you might want to adjust according to the circumstances, which means preparation is necessary. For example, if you're changing your menu and adding a Mongolian menu, instead of giving your "elevator" speech about how great your restaurant is, you might want to consider saying to a reporter whose interest you piqued that "Tommy's Place is the only restaurant in the state that offers a Mongolian Menu with a wide variety of beef, camel and vegetarian dishes. We can seat parties of two or 200." What you've done here is shown there is uniqueness to your restaurant, it can be a private or public affair, and you can accommodate beef eaters (and presumably other meat eaters) as well as vegetarians who are loath to eat animal flesh.

If you know that you have an impending interview and it's over the telephone, write the money quote down and keep it in front of you. Say it clearly and with enthusiasm. If the reporter is facing you, don't read it. Just memorize it. Even if you take the time to create a money quote, there's no guarantee the reporter will use it. But it's a good exercise in focusing your message, and if you give enough interviews, sooner or later it'll crop up in the media.

A True Story. As a reporter in Washington, D. C., I had tried for about a week to arrange an interview with a medical doctor. We finally managed to conduct the interview, and I filed the story. Not surprisingly, the editor had one or two more follow-up questions, a not uncommon occurrence, no matter how good the journalist. I called the doctor back to ask the questions and discovered he had gone to Africa for a few months (this was before the advent of e-mail). When you conclude your interview, mention casually if you're going to be on the road. Simply say, "If you have any follow-up questions, I'm going to be on the road on Thursday and Friday of this week but can be reached through e-mail or at The Plaza in New York." Then give the journalist your contact points, cell phone, assistant's phone number or e-mail address. ALWAYS be accessible. Sometimes that's the only thing that will get you published over your competition.

Always send the journalist some backup information whenever possible that might add to the story. It's helpful to know how journalists write. Most put their notes together, and when they've accumulated all the information, they begin to write. This is even true of newspaper reporters who have the most difficult (print) deadlines. A media kit is probably your best bet, though many are dreadful because they contain too much extraneous material. When you send information, ask if it's OK to send a story about you in a previous article, but don't offer an article that a competitor wrote, especially if it's recent (less than one year old) unless you're sure the information you've given in the interview is fresh. If you have any material that might add information or a fresh angle to the interview – an article in a trade journal, a Web site – don't hesitate to pass it on to the journalist, especially if he is a person you hope to cultivate. The journalist will appreciate and remember your gesture.

Always send the journalist a thank-you note. No one does, and believe me, they'll remember. Yes, they know you're kissing butt, but everyone except for those with the thickest behind appreciates it when someone appreciates them. Sure, everyone suggests sending a thank-you note. You've told yourself that it's a practice you intend to incorporate in your business. You've even bought nice note cards. Maybe even had custom note cards printed up. When's the last time you sent one?

I often send out art cards, beautiful reproductions of paintings from the Vatican art collection. Unless the person is an artistic troglodyte, they have to love the artwork even if they can't stand me.

Don't forget: Be yourself, say only what you won't mind seeing in print the next day, prepare a money quote and send a thank-you note. It's easy and effective.

A few thoughts about interviews.

My opposition [to interviews] lies in the fact that offhand answers have little value or grace of expression, and that such oral give and take helps to perpetuate the decline of the English language.
James Thurber, U.S. humorist, illustrator

. . .There aren't any embarrassing questions – just embarrassing answers.
Carl Rowan, U.S. Ambassador to Finland, journalist

Chapter 32

When To Get It Done

The Big– Medium– And Small–Bang Theory

There are a number of reasons that people establish a goal but then fail to achieve it. Sometimes the goal isn't clear or specific enough (get rich), which means they haven't thought it out carefully, and they probably haven't written it down. They lack a plan. Sometimes there is a plan, but the person simply fails to implement whatever plan he had for reaching his goal. In the information age, there is no excuse for not having a plan – even if it's a bad one. You can buy books (like this one), search the Internet, buy plans (my media plan costs $3,000) or, better yet, have a friend write the plan for free. (If they know what they're doing.) While plans are extremely important, failing to implement it is where most people stumble. Often, after stumbling, they never really pick themselves up. I'm not here to preach about goals or implementation, just to give you my assessment of what I find to be the reason so many publicity campaigns fail.

Hopefully by now you've identified the media you want to influence, and you also have a good sense of how you're going to do it. Now comes the task of actually implementing your plan. You have to have one realistic conversation with yourself about how you work, in other words, how you get things done. Are you methodical and virtuous about tasks on a daily basis? Do you enjoy doing things a little at a time and a little every day? Or do you prefer setting aside a time of day – or a day, week or even several weeks – and then work yourself into a frenzy of activity until you accomplish the task, usually within the range of an impending deadline?

You can take one of three approaches to implementing a publicity campaign. You can do a little bit every day, either counting the tasks or keeping track of the time (just like when it comes to writing). This is a "numbers" game which every salesperson recognizes. Make enough sales calls (pitches in your cases) and sooner or later – even if it's only through luck – your number will finally pop up and you'll get a media hit. Obviously before a major event, such as a grand opening or sponsoring a seasonal sale, you might have to ratchet up your efforts for the occasion. (If you intend to implement successfully, you're going to have to organize yourself. I highly recommend Mark H. McCormack's *Getting Results For Dummies*. You'll see immediate improvement.)

The next approach, the medium bang, is establishing several periods throughout the year where you tackle the issue of publicity for your business or organization. Saying that you'll devote two to three days each quarter is an excellent approach. What I would suggest is a special folder marked publicity ideas. Drop notes, story ideas and newspaper and magazine clips into that file for later use. Also create an electronic version of this folder. Then, when you sit down to decide what you're going to do, who you're going to contact and how you're going to implement it, your approach will be much clearer. For example, if you've noticed someone in the local paper writing about a business similar to yours, it might be wise to search the articles you saved and refer to them when you write or call the reporter. (You must be disciplined here, because what you don't want to do is "pass" when it comes time to think of publicity and say that you'll get to it in a couple of days, which then turns into the next quarter.) What makes sense is a quarterly assessment. I like this approach (for the nonprofessional) because you can prepare for it in advance. You conduct your mini-publicity campaign, and, when you're done, you go back to what you really do.

The last approach is the big bang. You simply drop everything you're doing and for a week or two devote yourself to a massive publicity effort every year or even every few years. Obviously, this effort must revolve around a huge event or special circumstance that justifies the time and money. At the very least, you must take this approach when you have a one-time special event. For example, my barbershop just celebrated its 100th anniversary as the oldest continuously opened barbershop in the same location in New Jersey. They had write-ups in local newspapers, received a proclamation and made the local TV news. My barber (in a previous life) learned something about getting publicity.

My suggestion is that, except for "special" or one-time events, you should always try for a stream of publicity on a regular basis, not just occasionally. As a former vice president of Procter & Gamble (which knows something about marketing and public relations) said, you want to make constant deposits in the mental banks of potential customers and clients.

However, even a once-a-year approach is better than no effort. Often the effects of your effort can be felt months down the road because of the carryover effects of a successful publicity campaign. I confess that the daily routine of seeking publicity is probably something you won't sustain because it's not what you do in your business. I think it's important, especially if you consider publicity or public relations under the rubric of marketing or communications, but most of us start with these daily gems of activities, and we drop them the minute "the job" or the client or customer needs something.

The reality is that the nature of your business, personal style and work ethic will dictate how you conduct yourself when dealing with what you'll follow naturally. My advice is to create a publicity-seeking schedule and stick to it. It almost doesn't matter whether you do it daily, monthly, quarterly or annually. It's the failure to have a plan or failing to follow through that is the ruin of more publicity campaigns than anything else.

A True Story. While I'm rewriting this chapter, an editor e-mailed me asking for an electronic version of an audit tip sheet I had sent more than six months ago. The tip sheet was about reducing costs in the manufacturing and distribution sector. This editor is now writing an article about women in manufacturing and wanted my tip sheet to run as a sidebar. There is something rewarding about making an effort towards publicity, then several weeks or months (sometimes years) later you get the phone call or note out of the blue for more information or maybe a photo request. It's always a sweet feeling.

Chapter 33

When To Hire A Public Relations Firm

Bring In The Artillery

When should you hire a public relations firm? **Never!** OK, I'm just kidding, but I want to needle my fellow flaks who might read this book.

A True Story. I worked for a major civic organization, my first "real" job after I left journalism. I came across an invoice that a public relations firm sent us for work on a particular campaign. I saw the billing rates of the senior vice president. I was standing as I read the invoice and almost fell back into my chair. Here's why. It wasn't the rate, though back then I couldn't believe you could bill as much as a lawyer – or more, sometimes. It's that on my worst day, I was better at working the media than this person was on her best day. That's not braggadocio. As Will Sonnett said; "No brag, just fact." I was stunned at the cost.

The reality is that unless you have lots of money, at least a nine-month commitment, with a year being the most realistic, you should forget about hiring a public relations firm to conduct a long-term strategic public relations campaign. Do it yourself. Here's why. I charge $150 an hour (in 2004), and those are modest rates given my client list and experience. That's $1,200 per day, and I **don't** take clients who only need me one day a month. I can't get enough done in a day – in most cases – to accomplish the client's goals. I look for long-term clients, not for someone who's with me for six months and then pulls out because the money dries up. That's why my clients are on the New York Stock Exchange or are small companies with more than 75 employees who are tops in their field but still relatively unknown. (Quick example: One of my clients designed 60 percent of the new malls that opened in the United States in 1999.) Occasionally, with a new firm on a tight budget, I've chosen to take stock options in lieu of cash. These days, however, I'm less inclined.

Why does this matter to you? If you hire a public relations firm, you'll be paying the cost of a salary for a lower-end assistant if you have a one-year commitment. If you can afford it, fine. Realistically, though, many small businesses and not-for-profits don't have that kind of money. Use my book, write a plan, follow through and you'll be fine.

The Plan, Boss, The Plan. If you still want to look for a public relations firm, ask them to give you a plan so that you can judge whether or not you'd be interested in hiring them. I give a one-page plan for free. My step-by-step plan costs $3,000. I don't charge for the plan if the person requesting it becomes a client. You've seen my comments about a plan throughout this book. What do you think I do when I'm feeling dull and unsure where to go with a client? I look at the plan that I drew up for the client and examine it for areas that have not received the attention they deserve from me. Then I increase my activity in those areas. Everyone loses focus at some point. The plan keeps you on the road. That's why we call it a plan.

Journalists. Why they're my favorite scoundrels. Try to get a handle on how the public relations firm feels about dealing with the media. Here's something most public relations people will never tell you. The portion of public relations that deals with the media – which means pitching stories and hoping, praying even, for getting your story to appear in a publication or getting on radio and TV – is called media relations. It's probably the least popular part of public relations. Many public relations people (those of you in PR can save the letters, I know this is true) hate that part of public relations. Why shouldn't they? It's mostly a system where you get a NO every day. You send out 100 press releases and follow up, and you're lucky if you get more than a few "hits". Then, too, journalists can be arrogant. A common complaint about journalists is that they are one-inch deep and one-mile wide. It is true to the degree that they touch, maybe superficially, on many topics. Yet in their defense it isn't as though the rest of the U.S. working population is laden with deep thinkers. I know, because I was a journalist. I still am. What I do love about journalists and why I went into the profession is that, all things being equal, they start and remain as honest as any profession I know. Proof of that is they often remain in the profession for far too long, making lousy wages compared to so many other fields. After a while, seeing your peers who are at least 20 points below you on the I.Q. scale making a great deal more money becomes irritating. So then you go into public relations and begin to charge those marvelous fees. Of course, it helps to be an expert.

There is another reason I like journalists, though most will choke on this when they read it: Journalists, for the most part, are as idealistic as any profession I know. Sure, time and life turn some cynical, but their desire to make a difference is what I find appealing about the profession.

I believe that my success as a publicity expert hinges on the fact that I still think more as a journalist than a public relations practitioner. As a joke, I created a business card that says, "Tom Peric', Crypto-journalist." When I'm in a particularly good mood, I pass out my "crypto-journalist" card.

Ah, yes, those media contacts. Don't put too much faith in someone telling you all about their alleged contacts in the media. Either the story that you're pitching is there, meaning it has news value as interpreted by the editor who's examining it so it will sell itself, or the news appeal is lacking, you don't have the story, and it's doubtful someone can make it magically appear in the media. Believe this: No magic wand on the part of a PR person is going to place a story in the media if there's no story, regardless of how great your public relations person's contacts are. Believe me, if you're not a big-time operation, you can't afford the few publicity people who really do have great contacts. This is akin to saying that you have $5,000 and want to get the best stockbroker in New York. Not likely. This doesn't mean, however, that on a local level, reasonably priced public relations experts lack good contacts. They might, and if your story is local, they might do a fine job. You need very deep pockets for a national campaign, and no matter how deep are your pockets, it's still the newsworthiness that matters most.

Who's Really In Charge Here? Be sure that when hiring a public relations firm to handle your business, you know exactly who handles your account. The larger the company, the further away the person who asked for your business will be when it comes time to implement the plan. For example, initially, you might be talking to a senior vice president who will ask for your business. However, it is unlikely that same person will be the one responsible for the day-to-day duties of pitching stories. At my company, Galileo Communications Inc., you get me. While I have six associates who work with me on various assignments, I personally pitch 99 percent of all my stories, which means you've hired the fastest gun in the East for the job. In major firms, if you're a large potential client, the company president, who bills $300 to $500 an hour, will turn your account over to some lower-level employee. How good will that employee be? Try flipping a coin or predicting the movement of the stock market. You might get lucky. You might not.

Confession Time. I have a major prejudice to confess. Without any hesitation, I would say the best public relations people who work in media relations invariably have been journalists themselves. Yes, I know that college kids who majored in public relations in college (what the hell were you thinking?) will cringe when they read this, but it's true. Of course, there are a few exceptions. There have been two occasions where public relations people fooled me because they had such a good grasp of how the media worked. I figured they had been journalists, but I was wrong. These types of PR people are rare. I can talk to most public relations people and usually tell within 10 to 15 minutes whether they've ever worked at a legitimate news organization for any length of time. My record output on a daily newspaper for one day was writing five stories in one day. I wrote only one of those stories from a press release. So when I tell you to understand the pressures of a newspaper reporter, I know what I'm talking about because I once felt that pain <u>and</u> the adrenaline rush of meeting a deadline.

A realistic low-budget plan for hiring a top gun. If your budget is modest and you're unsure what to do, talk to someone in PR (again, favor those who have been journalists) and ask them if they would charge you their hourly rate for a review of your plan. In other words, you write the plan and do all the heavy lifting. Put a limit on how much input you'll take. Let's say someone is willing to do this for you, charges $150 per hour and agrees to review the plan with suggestions and will stop the clock at four hours. That's not bad. You have $600 invested in professional public relations advice. I still give advice in this manner occasionally, but it drives me crazy when I give counsel on a plan and the person who paid me doesn't implement it at all or does it ineptly. Sure I have the fee, but personally? **I LOVE IT** when a plan comes together (to paraphrase actor George Peppard).

As a rule, I only take on clients who are willing to commit to at least nine months and two full days per month of my time for a public relations effort. The length of time is important because it takes a **minimum** of three to six months to see the benefits of most public relations campaigns. This doesn't apply to one-shot efforts – such as a store opening – but I seldom take those types of assignments any longer. I've also gotten media coverage for a campaign in less than three months, but that's unusual in print, far more probable in broadcast. After I give a speech or seminar, invariably someone asks me whether they could hire me for some consultation, yet they lack the funds for my minimal commitment. I usually have an uncomplicated answer. I suggest they:

- ❑ Read my book, *Wacky Days*, thoroughly.
- ❑ Read my book, *Wacky Days*, a second time.
- ❑ Draw up a plan.
- ❑ Implement the plan except for the actual mailing, phone calls and e-mail. In other words, create the media list, write the press release, prepare the follow-up, etc.
- ❑ Allow me to assess the plan.

This approach usually takes half a day to assess the plan. It allows someone like me who knows the publicity field to see if what you're doing is right and which mistakes to avoid. It also allows me to offer suggestions that you've never thought of and to remind you of some steps you might have missed. It costs a lot less than hiring me or some other public relations firm for a year. Keep a tight rein on your money, write a good plan and get the best advice you can afford. Reread my book. And then, put your plan into action.

Chapter 34

The Last Word

"Doesn't He Ever Shut Up?"

I wish there were a simple, clear, succinct "last word" that you could hold close to your publicity bosom and refer to when you're down and lonely, one that would nourish you during your publicity-attempt trials. Especially when you're going nowhere with your efforts. Unfortunately, there is no magic elixir, or I'd be sipping it every day as I read Andrew Tobias or The Wall Street Journal.

My ideas, suggestions and tactics really work. I know they work because I've used them for clients, and we've obtained millions of dollars in publicity. This is not an overnight solution. This is why reputable public relations firms often tell potential clients that a publicity campaign involving the media takes at least three to six months before you begin to see results.

I've listed the 10 commandments in the next chapter. They are the minimal steps or attitudes you must adopt if you wish to be successful. There is still one vexing problem. How much effort should you put into the project and how much should you exert yourself on behalf of one media source or outlet?

I posed a related question once to my friend Millionaire Mike in New York City. Now you have to know Millionaire Mike. He's from my hometown, but I didn't know him until I went to college. We stayed in touch after graduation and became closer as we became grayer.

I was mulling over how often I should call on a potential client. This was a BIG client, and I still hadn't hit my stride, so I wanted to pitch my business like crazy. I knew that Millionaire Mike was an incredible salesman. He would have the answer.

A True Story. I'm walking with Millionaire Mike in New York City, and he points to a tall skyscraper – a bank – and he says to me, "I sold them more than $1 billion in bonds." Now you know why I call him Millionaire Mike. He's driven, very smart, a jugular sort of guy who cuts through the muck and goes to the heart of the matter. And he's still relatively young.

I'm anguishing over the issue of how often to call on a potential client. What is too much effort (you waste time because it's better to cut bait and go pitch someone else) or quitting too soon (when one more call closes the deal and you get a media hit)? I decided to ask Millionaire Mike. I mean, if he doesn't have the answer, who does?

Of course, what I was looking for was absolution. I wanted Millionaire Mike to say, "Stop after two calls," or "Stop after nine calls." The answer didn't really matter – I just wanted a figure so that if I met it and then stopped, I wouldn't feel like I was quitting.

After posing the question, Millionaire Mike said without any hesitation, "It depends on how important the potential client is." Now you know why he made a lot more money than me. Because that is the answer.

That's exactly the formula you must use when weighing your time and effort against the intensity of pitches you hurl at the media. There isn't any easy formula that works exactly the same each time. You must decide the importance of the publicity campaign and the specific efforts directed to any media outlet. In some cases, you might NEVER follow up, never send a tip sheet, just a press release a few times each year. In other cases, you might cultivate a reporter and meet with that person once a month. (Always bring story ideas that don't affect you and that are not self-serving.) You might even become friends with the reporter. Recognizing what's important and how much effort to expend is vitally important in any successful publicity campaign (and many other endeavors, too). Indeed, I've had clients who could do a fairly credible job themselves, but they don't want to . . . so they hired me.

Follow these rules and I know you'll gain more publicity than you've ever thought possible. Woody Allen hit it close to the mark when he said something to the effect that a big part of winning was "just showing up." I'm amazed at how often that's the case.

The Absolute Last Word: When in doubt about your entire approach, remember that your pitch must address the issue of how your idea is interesting, useful, relevant or entertaining to the audience. You must be able to explain to a journalist why your ideas are important and why they're important NOW. Don't forget how essential your media list is. Does it fit what they're looking for? And after that, indeed, maybe before that, is one irrefutable adage: It's always about people and ideas. That's it in a nutshell. It's about people and ideas. Pitch that regularly and you'll pitch yourself into the arms and heart of a waiting journalist and a shower of publicity. Good luck.

A few thoughts about the last word (advice).

There is nothing which we receive with so much reluctance as advice.
Joseph Addison, English essayist, poet and politician

Advice is like snow; the softer it falls, the longer it dwells upon, and the deeper it sinks into the mind.
Samuel Taylor Coleridge, English writer

Chapter 35

The 10 Commandments Of Publicity

Sin No More – 10 Invaluable Reminders When Mounting A Publicity Campaign

1. **It's Only About Two Things.** People and ideas, that's the key. Get your people factor or the importance of the idea you're pitching right, and you'll make headway against your competition for media attention. Without hesitating, you must always be able to answer why your story is important and why it is important *now*.
2. **The Who?** Creating or using the right media list is crucial unless you're going after the broadest possible media target. You **must** focus on the media list if you want the press to pick up your story. No matter how great an idea or human element you have, if they don't cover the angle you're pitching, it won't work. Make a realistic appraisal of which journalists you really want to influence. Virtually every businessman I meet says he wants to be in *The Wall Street Journal*. It's a great ego-booster, but what makes <u>your</u> story so special? For small businesses, a local weekly or daily newspaper or

an important trade publication is both realistic and can be just as profitable. I can't say this too often.

3. **Watch Or Read The News.** I've always thought one of the craziest (and arrogant) statements I've ever heard is when someone says they want to write a book, but they don't read books. If you never watch or read the news, you'll never develop a sense of how the media interprets and reports a story.
4. **It Never Ends.** Think of publicity as a work-in-progress. I tell this to clients frequently. No matter how high you feel when you get a media hit, it will turn cool and fade within days. I would rather have a client in the media throughout the year, a small splash here and there, than one big splash which no one remembers two months later. News applies to the *now*, not what happened six months ago, no matter how important.
5. **The Friday Phone Call.** Maybe the best advice I ever heard from a public relations person. Once a week, make it a Friday whenever possible (people are more relaxed), make one cold call to a journalist. By the end of the year, you should have made at least 45 calls (that allows you seven weeks of vacation). Then tell me that you didn't get one media hit. You also might have made some contacts, learned something about a media outlet and maybe even made a new friend.
6. **Enthusiasm Works**. When you're pitching your idea or story, and your enthusiasm, yes, even passion, shows through, it'll make that editor wonder why. You can even do this with your writing if you have the skill. I remember an editor e-mailing me with the line, "I don't usually answer pitches for a few weeks but just had to . . ." Just be sure you can back up all your claims.
7. **Don't Take It Personally**. Don't take it personally when someone doesn't run your press release. There are literally dozens of reasons why a news organization might decide to pass on your story. In most cases, you'll never know the real reason. This is a game where

(unless you're an established public figure or celebrity) you'll mostly get rejection. Forget about it. It's nothing personal.

8. **Create Your Own Idea Folder**. Remember my insistence about how important this folder was to a journalist? Turn it around to benefit you. Whenever you see, hear or watch a journalist covering a story, especially if you can see the follow-up, be sure to make a note of it and follow up. I have a traditional idea folder in a file cabinet and an electronic one.
9. **The X Factor**. Sometimes the Lord and the stars decide it won't happen in your favor. No matter how carefully you plan, something goes awry. No one in this publicity business hits 100 percent. If some of the top pros in the business strike out, so can you. Even baseball's top hitters make an out 7 out of 10 times up.

   Just be sure that it was circumstances beyond your control that contributed to the fizzle and not your effort, strategy or tactics. The solution? Come back and try again.
10. **Be Honest, Fair And Thoughtful**. This is the 10 Commandments, after all. If you are in the game long enough, some people, especially the journalists and media people to whom you're pitching, will form opinions about you. Better that they think you're someone they can trust and rely upon for truthfulness and accuracy than snake oil and hyperbole. And volunteer some of these newly found publicity skills for a worthy cause.

A few thoughts about rules.

Honest advice is unpleasant to the ears.
Chinese proverb

Call them rules or call them limits, good ones, I believe, have this in common: They serve reasonable purposes; they are practical and within a child's capability; they are consistent; and they are an expression of loving concern.
Mr. Fred Rogers, U.S. television personality and parenting specialist

Chapter 36

Help Beyond These Pages...

At Your Service

I often read books and think, "Hey, I'd like to get in touch with the author about what was said on page..." but then I figure they're too busy, don't care, are on an island, whatever. Well, I am generally not on an island, but am (thankfully) quite busy, mostly due to the needs of others. Like you, perhaps.

I am available for publicity or editorial consulting. I also give seminars on publicity, entitled Publicity For Profit. I enjoy nothing more than writing, speaking and teaching. This passion was the fuel for the book.

However, please know that while I can usually handle speaking assignments, I often get calls or e-mails from people who need assistance on short notice. (I've built my life around short deadlines, but please don't make your crisis mine!) Give me some time to respond since I can't sacrifice a current client's project deadlines for new business. If you were a client, that's how you would want to be treated.

Just call or e-mail and we can either work out a solution right then to help you out or schedule a convenient time for both of us.

Thanks so much, and I look forward to hearing from you.

Contact:
T.S. "Tom" Peric'
2040 Fairfax Avenue
Cherry Hill, NJ 08003
(856-874-0049) • (856-874-0052) fax
tom@wackydays.com

A few thoughts about help.

Help me, Obi Wan Kenobi. You're my only hope.
Princess Leia (Carrie Fisher, *Star Wars*, message sent on a hologram of Leia and carried by robot R2D2)

We all want to help one another. Human beings are like that.
Charlie Chaplin, British actor, screenwriter and director

Chapter 37

More Free Publicity

The Publicity For Profit Report

I know what you're thinking. There's no such thing as "free." Always a gimmick, always a catch. If you think like that, well, you have the makings of a good journalist.

People frequently ask me for new tips or fresh versions of familiar ideas for getting publicity. In short, they want to know more than what's found in these pages. And they want a dose of inspiration as they wage their effort to get the word out about themselves or their products and services.

Here's my offer. You can subscribe, for free, to my monthly electronic newsletter, *The Publicity For Profit Report*. It's monthly, it's free (honest) and it's tight and bright. I won't ramble and I won't spend half of my newsletter pitching products or services that I want to sell you.

And I'll NEVER sell or rent my newsletter list to anyone. Period. It's as simple as that. Once a month, a fresh dose of ideas from Tom Peric'. (By the way, the apostrophe after my name announces a "ch" sound. The pronunciation is "Pear-Rich." It's Croatian.)

If you want to opt in for the e-newsletter, send a request to me at tom@wackydays.com. If you want a monthly hard copy, it'll cost you $99 for an annual subscription.

Appendix

Here's a copy of an Adams Hudson press release. I've included the third draft we marked up with corrections. According to my records, the final draft (the clean copy you see) was the 11th! That's slightly deceptive because I wasn't on a time crunch when I reworked the release. Often I'll change only a paragraph or two (or even a few words) and save it as the next draft. I consider the final piece a very tight press release. Important note: We changed the slug (the placement of the contact information so that journalists can reach you), and this release was "tight" in the sense that we intended to keep it to one page. Two-page press releases are acceptable, but for a variety of reasons we chose one page for this campaign. Thus we really had to stretch the margins, and the headline was not nearly as large as I like it. But the best part about this no-frills release is that it worked. Press releases are NOT works of art. They are simply tools to be used and then discarded until the next one. I've also included a Guest Alert (and Media Alert) and a PSA.

NEWS RELEASE

Contact: Kenny Lignon (kenny@hudsonink.com)
Hudson, Ink
1-800-489-9099
313 North Hull Street
Montgomery, AL 36104

Make More Money With Free HVAC Marketing Calendar or Free Calendar Helps Solve HVACR Marketing Headaches ~~Solve Your Marketing Problems With Free HVACR . . .~~

“What do I do next?” ~~is what marketing expert Adams Hudson says~~ is ~~the number one question is~~ the No. 1 question that marketing expert Adams Hudson hears. ~~he receives~~. “Contractors are looking for a marketing plan” ~~he continues,~~ “because ~~that~~ most admit they just don’t have one, ~~sadly~~ one doesn’t exist for most of them,~~.~~” Hudson said.

More contractors have disaster plans than marketing plans. Hudson 88% of contractors he surveyed admitted to having no real marketing plan. As a result, contractors run his ads, get the leads, close the sales and *then* to figure out the next step.”

“This borders on ~~is~~ criminal business behavior,” Hudson said. “When ~~especially when~~ you consider that the 4-6% of gross revenue that contractors spend on marketing is responsible for virtually all of their new customer leads and sales,” he ~~. Having~~said.” Having a plan – with specific marketing tools to use – is a gold mine in time spent and profit made.”

~~So~~ Hudson Ink has compiled a free, comprehensive and useful ~~a free, useful and comprehensive put together a full-fledged~~ 2002 Marketing Calendar for contractors. It shows the "Marketing Focus" for each month, along with "Media Watch" recommendations and even what to look out for in upcoming months.

Included on the calendar are such tips as:

- **The 32 days a year you should never mail sales letters. (December 10- January 12.)**
- **The worst newspaper day is generally the one the rep recommends. (Sunday.)**
- **A postage technique that reduces cost but increases your response. (Called "Live, standard.")**
- **How to drop your newspaper rate but increase your company's recognition with small, cheap ads. (Called a "TOMA" program. Proven to work at minimal cost.)**
- **How to multiply your Tune-Up leads by 2.8 times. (A call-behind campaign with the right 3-sentence script.)**

"There are many seasonal marketing strategies on this calendar that no ad agency would ever know," Hudson ~~.~~ ~~This~~said. "This calendar is for contractors only."

You can get the 2002 HVAC Marketing calendar – which ~~is~~ is attractively ~~nicely~~ printed with handsome photography and "wall-ready" – by faxing Hudson, Ink your letterhead with the request to 334-262-1115. You may also visit www.hudsonink.com **or call them at 1-800-489-9099.**

"Simply having a plan is far better than no plan," Hudson **says. "And with this calendar, you have both a plan and a way to increase sales."~~can now say you have one!~~"**

END

Note: This release was issued on a single sheet of paper. This was the third version of the press release.

NEWS RELEASE

Contact: Kenny Lignon (kenny@hudsonink.com)
Hudson, Ink
1-800-489-9099
313 North Hull Street
Montgomery, AL 36104

Free Calendar Helps Contractors Solve HVACR Marketing Headaches

"What do I do next?" is the No. 1 question that marketing expert Adams Hudson hears. "Contractors are looking for a marketing plan because most admit they just don't have one," Hudson said.

More contractors have disaster plans than marketing plans. Hudson said 88% of contractors he surveyed admitted to having "no real marketing plan." As a result, contractors run the ads he creates, get the leads, close the sales and *then* try to figure out the next step.

"This is a terrible business approach that will either doom your business or permanently lower your profits, especially when you consider that most contractors spend 4 – 6% of their gross revenues on marketing," Hudson said. "This budget is responsible for virtually all of a contractor's new leads and sales. Having a plan – with specific marketing tools to use – is a gold mine in time spent and profit made."

Hudson, Ink has compiled a free, comprehensive and useful 2002 Marketing Calendar for contractors. It shows the "Marketing Focus" for each month, along with "Media Watch" recommendations and even what to look out for in upcoming months.

Tips from the calendar, with many seasonal strategies only for contractors, include:

- The 32 days a year you should never mail sales letters. (Dec. 10 - Jan. 12.)
- The worst newspaper day is generally the one the rep recommends. (Sunday.)
- A postage technique that reduces cost but increases your response. (Called "Live, standard.")
- How to drop your newspaper rate but increase your company's recognition with small, cheap ads. (Called a "TOMA" program. Proven to work at minimal cost.)
- How to multiply your Tune-Up leads by 2.8 times. (A call-behind campaign with the right three-sentence script.)

You can get the 2002 HVAC Marketing calendar – which is attractively printed with handsome photography and "wall-ready" – by faxing Hudson, Ink your letterhead with the request to 334-262-1115. You may also visit www.hudsonink.com or call them at 1-800-489-9099.

"Simply having a plan is far better than no plan," Hudson says. "And with this calendar, you have both a plan and a way to increase sales."

END

Note: This release was issued on a single sheet of paper. This was the final version of the press release.

SAMPLE

GUEST ALERT

WHO: Frank Petersen, Ph.D., founder of The American Institute For The Promotion Of Chess In Schools.

WHAT: World Record Breaking Attempt For Playing Blindfold Chess.

WHEN: April 5 – 6, 2001, at 12 p.m. (Noon) Dr. Petersen will give a five-minute intro about blindfold chess before beginning.

WHERE: Washington Square, New York City.

WHY IS THIS IMPORTANT:

Playing chess improves learning and grades. Several studies repeat the same conclusion. Students who learn chess and play competitively do better in school, score higher on tests and improve their self-image. Dr. Petersen will play 50 opponents at the same time, without the use of any chessboards. He will be "blind."

HOW: Give us a call, and we'll arrange a telephone interview with Dr. Petersen.

FINAL WORD:

Chess helps make kids smarter. They enjoy the thrill of mastering a skill. This demonstration will provide plenty of opportunities for interviews and video including shots of adults and children playing chess. Parents and kids will be eager to see how Dr. Petersen plays (and wins) at blindfold chess.

CONTACT: Tom Peric' 856-874-0049

Note: When I'm pitching an event, I use the term "MEDIA ALERT."

Public Service Announcement (Sample)

Your Favorite School System
1111 The Old School House
Tyler, TX 00000
(903) 555-0000
(903) 555-0000 (fax)

Public Service Announcement
NOMINATIONS FOR THE BEST CITY EMPLOYEE

From: Jane Smith
School Superintendent

For Use: 10 SECONDS – Jan. 1, 2004, through Jan. 7, 2004

NOMINATE THE BEST CITY EMPLOYEE
IN TYLER, TEXAS
FOR A $5,000 AWARD
CALL FIVE-FIVE-FIVE-ZERO-ZERO-ZERO-ZERO*
TO REQUEST A NOMINATION FORM TODAY
*If your area uses multiple area codes, include the correct one in the telephone portion of your PSA.

Bibliography

People often ask me what books I read or keep handy in my office. Here are some of the books resting above my computer or on the bookshelf behind me. This is not an exhaustive list. However, most of these have served me well through the years.

Agee, William Kendall, et. al. **Introduction to Mass Communications**. I have an old, 1994 edition, but this provides a good overview of mass communications. Get a more recent copy because my version doesn't mention the Internet.

Associated Press. **The Associated Press Stylebook and Libel Manual**. The bible.

Bernstein, Theodore, M. **The Careful Writer**. Index style when you have a word- or grammar-related question. Many journalists regard this book as a classic.

Bly, Robert. **The Elements of Copywriting**. A small, tight, focused book. Superb as a reminder of what you should do when writing copy, without overwhelming you with suggestions.

Fowler, W. H. **Modern English Usage**. A classic. Makes me feel important to have this famous work on the English language.

Kamoroff, Bernard B. C.P.A. **422 Tax Deductions**. If you own a business (even if you operate it part-time), this is must reading. Too bad there aren't 1,000 deductions.

Kremer, John. **1,001 Ways to Market Your Books**. If you've written a book to establish your expertise but don't know how to market it, this is the guide you need. It simply overflows with creative, practical advice.

Kremer, John. **Celebrate Today**. More than 3,000 reasons to celebrate throughout the year. I also have the CD, which has a listing of more than 10,000. You can mine this for more publicity.

McCormack, Mark H. **On Selling**. I'm a lousy salesperson, but if selling is your business, McCormack is brilliant in avoiding hyperbole and fads. He's one of the most clear-headed writers on business topics I've ever read. He started his business, IMG, with $500 and turned it into a billon-dollar enterprise, so he offers much more than theory. (His corporate offices are across the street from one of my most important clients.)

Oxford University Press. **The Concise Oxford Dictionary**. I love how the British spell. Doesn't honourable seem more sophisticated than honorable? Great for translating those British terms that pop up in English mysteries.

Poynter, Dan. **The Self-Publishing Manual: How to Write, Print and Sell Your Own Book**. Only an idiot would try to self-publish before reading this book. It will save you tons of money and hours of heartache. If you intend to self-publish and don't get a copy, you'll regret it.

Rosner, Bob. **Working Wounded**. If you're a boss, you must own a copy of this book. If you are an employee, you must own a copy. Full disclosure: Bob, a best-selling author, was my college roommate. Same advice applies to his book, **The Boss's Survival Guide.**

Seitel, Fraser P. **The Practice of Public Relations**. A popular college textbook on the subject. It gives a fine overview of the field.

Silbiger, Steven. **The Ten Day MBA Program**. Read this book (a chapter a day) and you have (sorta) an MBA in 10 days. Learn to make sense of MBA-speak.

Strunk, William Jr. and White, E. B. **The Elements of Style**. The best small book on the rules of English ever written. Period.

Tarshis, Barry. **Grammar for Smart People**. Makes the rules of English that you'll probably encounter clear even if you're not smart.

Tobias, Andrew. **The Only Investment Guide You'll Ever Need.** Do you think I write only for the fun? Of course. But when I think about what to do with what I earn, this is the book. Buy it.

Zinsser, William. **On Writing Well**. The best book I've ever read about how to write nonfiction. Case closed. (Much of it applies to fiction, too.)

A few thoughts about books.

The man who doesn't read good books has no advantage over the man who can't read them.
Mark Twain, U.S. humorist, writer & humorist

When I am attacked by gloomy thoughts, nothing helps me so much as running to my books. They quickly absorb me and banish the clouds from my mind.
Michel de Montaigne, French essayist

About The Author

Tom Peric' is president of Galileo Communications Inc., a communications consulting firm that specializes in creating editorial products and initiating aggressive public relations campaigns for clients. He also conducts *Publicity For Profit* seminars to boost business and not-for-profits toward maximum publicity possible at the lowest cost.

Tom's client list includes the largest developer of embedded software in the world, the 25th largest privately held company in the United States, the 12th largest investor-owned utility in the United States, the third largest business-to-business publisher in the United States, and a major utility company whose stock trades on the New York Stock Exchange, and the Republic of Croatia.

He forged his editorial expertise with a decade-long stint as a senior reporter in Washington, D.C. His experience includes serving as a business editor of a daily newspaper and various senior editorial positions on a variety of magazines. He helped launch editorial products for two client publications, one of the largest-circulation magazines focusing on small business in the United States (*Managing Small Business* magazine) and another for the mechanical contracting and wholesale industry. Tom is also a multi-award-winning journalist and publisher of the online newsletter, *The Publicity For Profit Report*.

In the public relations field, he is known for obtaining remarkable results with his media relations campaigns. One client with a national practice had less than $10,000 worth of media coverage annually before enlisting Tom's assistance. In less than two years, his publicity program garnered the client more than **$1.4 million in media coverage**. In the process, he turned one of the company's principals into the most published writer in his industry (excluding professional writers or columnists).

Tom was born in a refugee camp in Europe and immigrated to the United States as a child. He opened his first business at 19. He sold it several years later and attended The American University in Washington, D.C., on several academic scholarships, including a Scripps-Howard National Journalism Scholarship. He studied communications and history as an undergraduate and international affairs as a graduate student (summa cum laude).

Tom has extensive teaching experience as an instructor of writing and as a speaker on how the media works. He has taught at the University of Maryland, the University of Akron, Lakeland (Ohio) Community College and Camden County (New Jersey) College.

He started Galileo Communications Inc. in 1997. It has offices in Cherry Hill, NJ and Cleveland, Ohio.

Tom lives in Haddonfield, N.J. with his wife, Cheryl Federline, a Spanish teacher at the junior and senior high levels and formerly an international trade expert. They have a son, Andrew Paul.

Index

Book Order Form

Wacky Days: How to Get Millions of $$$ In Free Publicity by Creating A "Real" Holiday & Other Tactics Used by Media Experts

Fax Orders: 856-874-0052. Send this form.
Telephone Orders: Call 866-WACKYDAYS (922-5932) toll free
E-mail Orders: orders@wackydays.com
Postal Orders: Gregson & Lestrade, Publishers
2040 Fairfax Ave.
Cherry Hill, NJ 08003, USA.
Telephone: 856-874-0049

Cost per book: $19.95

Name ____

Address ____

City ________________________ State ______ Zip __________

Sales Tax: Please add 6% for products shipped to New Jersey addresses.

Shipping by Air

U.S.: $4.00 for first book or disk and $2.00 for each additional product.
International: $10.00 for first book or disk;
$5.00 for each additional product.

Payment: Check ☐ VISA ☐ MasterCard ☐

Card Number: ______________________________________

Name on Card: ______________________________________

Expiration Date ____________

Please send me more free information about:

Speaking & Seminars ☐ Consulting ☐